In *Peace* and *War*

The True Story of a Maritime Union's Fight for Democracy

DAVID WHITELEY

Copyright © 2025 by David Whiteley

All rights reserved. No portion of this publication may be reproduced, stored in an electronic system, or transmitted in any form by any means, electronic, mechanical, photocopy, recording, or otherwise, without the author's prior permission, except with brief quotations used in literary reviews and specific non-commercial uses permitted by copyright law. For permission requests, please contact Harvest Creek Publishing & Design at info@harvestcreek.net.

The views expressed in this book are the author's and do not necessarily reflect those of the publisher.

Every effort has been made to ensure that all the information in this book is accurate at the time of publication. The author can't control the validity of web addresses or information after publication.

Book Cover & Layout by Harvest Creek Publishing & Design
www.harvestcreek.net

Ordering Information: Groups, associations, and others can receive discounts on quantity purchases. For details, please contact the author directly using the information listed at the back of the book.

In Peace and War—1st ed.

ISBN: 978-1-961641-42-6

Printed in the United States of America

Contents

Dedication 5

Acknowledgments 7

Preface 9

The U.S. Merchant Marine: A Brief History 12

Jesse Calhoon 23

Along Came DeFries 38

Time to Get MAD 50

Suddenly Susan 63

In a Flash . . . Gordon 72

Dog Catches Car 98

Enough! 121

Back to the Future 130

Trials and Tribulations 141

Epilogue 152

About the Author 156

Dedication

This book is dedicated to
Diane Whiteley,
my wife for over 50 years,
who inspired me to write this book,
and to
Lawrence H. O'Toole,
my mentor and friend,
who also provided most of the documentation.
Acta Non Verba

Acknowledgments

First and foremost, thanks to Larry O'Toole for providing hundreds of documents and several photographs related to the MAD Committee and its fight to save the union and the pension. Without his boxes of documents, this book would not be possible.

Many thanks to:

- Don McLendon for providing background on the formation of the MAD Committee, and also some videos that were important for fleshing out the book.
- Curtis Calhoon, who was very generous with information and photographs about his father, Jesse Calhoon.
- Kurt A. Richwerger, who works at the Association for Union Democracy. He also provided valuable information and videos.
- Captain Ed Carr, who is writing a book on the LNG ships, offered some overlap information that he could provide. Thank you especially for the ETC Arbitration documents.
- Alex Shandrowsky, Mark Austin, and Louie Coulson (a Kings Point classmate) for providing interviews about the formation of the MAD Committee.
- Marco Cannistraro, who works in the MEBA Washington, D.C. headquarters. He could access the union archives and fill in a few holes. He also provided photographs from the archives.

Finally, I thank my wife, Diane, who encouraged me to write the book. She also collated all of Larry O'Toole's documents. First, she separated them into stacks by year. Then, she took each year and organized them chronologically by date from January to December. Finally, she punched each page and put them into binders labeled by year. It would have been impossible to write the book without such specific organizational tasks being completed!

Preface

*Son, I may have long left the sea . . .
But the sea has never left me.*
SHIPMATES REUNITED

★ WHEN I DECIDED to write this book, the idea was to write about my life during the sea years and tell the story of how I moved to the top of my field. One event that triggered my promotion was a merger between two unions that didn't seem quite right and caused a group of ship officers to form the MAD Committee to fight the merger. This was going to be a small part of the book.

While I was writing, I spoke with Larry O'Toole, a mentor and friend, and the chief engineer on my ship during the time the MAD Committee was doing battle. He was a major player in the fight and told me he had saved boxes of documents related to the merger. He invited me to his home in Connecticut, where the documents were stored in his barn.

When I got there, I found dozens of boxes filled with loose, disorganized papers related to the merger, including court documents, letters, memos, newspaper and magazine clippings, and flyers. I even found an affidavit signed by my brother, John, who also worked at sea and was a member of the licensed officers' union, MEBA. I left with hundreds of documents, a stack over one foot high.

The more I read about the merger and subsequent battle, the more amazed I was at how close we came to losing our pension plan and other union benefits. I also learned how the union leadership had modified the union's constitution and bylaws, shifting power from the union membership to the leadership, heading toward an autocracy. They had also used their power to line their pockets with millions of dollars. The more documents I read, the more I realized how similar this union fight was to the political issues currently unfolding in our country.

I scrapped the book about *my* life at sea and shifted to a book about the change in union leadership and the subsequent fight to save the pension. The book is factual and based entirely on documents retrieved from Larry O'Toole, Capt. Ed Carr (who is writing a book on LNG ships), Curtis Calhoon (son of Jesse Calhoon), and the Internet. The formation of the MAD Committee is not well-documented, as they didn't keep meeting minutes. I depended on interviews with Don McLendon, Alex Shandrowsky, Mark Austin, and Louie Coulson. And, of course, I was an active union member and had personal experience related to the fight to save the pension.

David Whiteley

Lord, stand beside the men who sail

Our merchant ships in storm and gale.

In peace and war, their watch they keep

On every sea, on thy vast deep.

Be with them, Lord, by night and day

For Merchant Mariners, we pray.

Chapter 1

The U.S. Merchant Marine: A Brief History

> *When final victory is ours, there is no organization that will share its credit more deservedly than the Merchant Marine.*
> GENERAL DWIGHT D. EISENHOWER

★ THE MARITIME INDUSTRY comprises merchant ships transporting goods between nations via oceans and waterways, as well as the shore-side infrastructure that supports them. The Second Continental Congress established a Continental Navy in 1775, but the Navy was disbanded after the Revolutionary War. According to the article "History of the United States Navy," found on Wikipedia, President George Washington reestablished the U.S. Navy under the Naval Act of 1794 with the sole purpose of protecting merchant shipping from Barbary pirates. Think about it; the merchant marine was so vital to the U.S. economy that the U.S. Navy was reestablished with the specific purpose of protecting it!

Early merchant vessels were powered by wind and sails; however, in 1787, John Fitch launched the first successful trial run of a steamboat, which took place on the Delaware River. In 1807, Robert Fulton and Robert R. Livingston developed the first commercially successful steamboat, known as the *Clermont*. This information can be found in the article "Career in the United States (1806-1815)" by Robert Fulton on Wikipedia.

Clermont had a 24-horsepower steam engine and paddle wheels on each side. She also had two small sails, one on the bow and one on the stern. *Clermont* was used to transport passengers between New York City and Albany via the Hudson River. By the time of the Civil War (1861-1865), wooden sailing ships were still in use by the Navy, but steam-powered vessels were also being employed by both the North and the South. The most famous battle was between the USS *Monitor* and the Confederate *Merrimack;* both ships were ironclads and powered by steam engines.

The increased use of steam engines in merchant ships had created a need for engine mechanics (called engineers) to operate and maintain the steam plant. In 1838, Congress enacted the Steamboat Act, which was somewhat vague and inefficient. In 1852, they enhanced the Steamboat Act to require a license to work on steamboats and enforced an inspection system. The Marine Engineers Beneficial Association (MEBA) was established in 1875 to represent licensed engineers and is the oldest union serving marine engineers. Refer to the "Marine Engineers' Beneficial Association" on Wikipedia for more information about the history of MEBA. It is still an active union and is one of the largest and most successful maritime unions in the world.

During World War I, the MEBA membership grew to 22,000 members. After the war, the U.S Shipping Board, led by Admiral William S. Benson, demanded that seagoing unions drastically cut wages, eliminate overtime pay, and reduce manning. By 1934, the membership had fallen to 4,848. By the time of the Great Depression, the U.S. merchant fleet had fallen far behind that of other nations. These statistics and more are available on the MEBA union website (*www.MEBAunion.org/about-us/MEBA-history*).

Congress passed the Merchant Marine Act of 1920, also known as the Jones Act, named after its sponsor, Sen. Wesley Jones. The law required that any ship entering two U.S. ports consecutively had to be a U.S.-flagged ship, constructed in the U.S., and owned by U.S. citizens. Every member of the crew must be a U.S. citizen possessing U.S. documentation, such as an engineer's license. This was intended to increase the number of U.S.-flagged ships and, with it, the number of U.S. merchant mariners.

The Jones Act also improved conditions for merchant mariners. Previously, if a mariner was injured and needed to be taken off the ship and hospitalized, the ship would sail, and the mariner was on their own, no matter where they were in the world. The Jones Act gave mariners who suffer personal injury the right to sue the company, captain, or other crewmembers. Shipping companies provided better care for the crew to avoid lawsuits. Pay was also an issue, and sometimes when a mariner returned to the U.S. and was signing off the ship, the shipping company would reduce the pay owed to the mariner by charging him for room and board or other services.

The Jones Act instituted shipping commissioners. When the ship returned to the U.S. and the crew was signing off, they would do so in front of the shipping commissioner. He was required by law to ask each person if they were satisfied with their pay. If a crew member was not satisfied for any reason, the shipping commissioner would investigate and determine the appropriate pay, ensuring that each crew member received full pay.

Sixteen years later, Congress revised the Jones Act with the Merchant Marine Act of 1936. The Jones Act now includes laws for a Construction Differential Subsidy (Subchapter V) and a Vessel Operating Assistance Subsidy (Subchapter VI). These subsidies were limited to ships operating in foreign trade. They were intended to subsidize U.S. companies, enabling them to compete with foreign companies that had lower operating costs.

President Roosevelt declared war on December 7, 1941, after the bombing of Pearl Harbor, and the need for ships and personnel to operate the ships in both the Atlantic and the Pacific increased dramatically. The U.S. Congress authorized the establishment of a school for ship officers, both deck officers and engineers. A few states already had state-funded maritime schools; however, in 1942, the War Shipping Administration bought the estate of deceased car manufacturer Walter P. Chrysler in Kings Point, New York. Buildings were constructed on the estate, and on September 30, 1943, Roosevelt dedicated the U.S. Merchant Marine Academy (aka Kings Point), the fourth Federal Military Academy.

Due to the war and the urgent need for ships' officers, Kings Point was truncated from a four-year education to an 18-month program, including six months actually working as an intern or midshipman aboard a merchant ship to gain practical experience. During World War II, 142 midshipmen were killed before graduation while working aboard ships operating in the war zones. After the war, Kings Point was restored to a four-year education with graduates receiving a B.S. Degree in either nautical science or marine engineering.

From 1942 to 1945, the U.S. built over 2700 Liberty Ships and 534 Victory Ships to transport goods into the war zones. The number of jobs available in MEBA increased to 200,000. Crossing the oceans in non-military ships was so dangerous that the Liberty and Victory ships were built cheaply and in large quantities, assuming that they might make only one voyage. According to Terri Moon Cronk of the *DOD News* dated May 19, 2022, the mortality rate for the U.S. Merchant Marine was 1 in 26, which was higher than any other branch of the U.S. military. Other crew members of the ships that sank were captured as prisoners of war.

During the Eisenhower administration, Congress amended the Jones Act once again by passing the Cargo Preference Act of 1954. This new law gave preferential treatment to U.S. ships when transporting U.S. government-sponsored cargoes overseas. When the U.S. Government was shipping aid or supplies to foreign countries, 50% of the cargo was required to be transported on U.S.-flagged ships. The percentage was increased to 75% for specific agricultural export programs. *The Journal of Maritime Law and Commerce,* Vol. 39, No. 3, from July 2008, provided these statistics.

After the war, the Maritime Administration (MARAD) began granting subsidies to companies that built ships meeting the requirements necessary for wartime operation. One of the MARAD requirements was that passenger cabins were to carry twelve passengers. These were required to house a small group of Navy personnel to protect the ship in the event it was used to support the military during a war, similar to the merchant marine's support in World War II.

In the 1960s, the C-4 class of ship was the first type of U.S.-flagged ship to be automated. It was now possible on this type of ship to open and close valves, as well as start and stop pumps, remotely from a console. MEBA opposed automation because they saw it as a means to reduce the crew size; they didn't want to eliminate any jobs. This was ironic because the Vietnam War was growing and would soon require hundreds of ships to supply the military. The industry would require more ship officers, not fewer.

By the mid-60s, the Vietnam War created a shortage of licensed officers, both mates and engineers. For two years, 1966 and 1967, Kings Point graduated midshipmen ten weeks early to help fill the void. Jesse Calhoon, president of MEBA, established "Operation LEAP" (Licensed Engineers Apprentice Program) as a way to help address the shortage of licensed engineers. The program was renamed Calhoon MEBA Engineering School in 1966 and became a two-year initiative, including six months at sea, aimed at addressing the shortage of licensed engineers. The first class, comprising 19 young men, graduated in October 1968. The program later expanded to three years, with one full year at sea working as a cadet. More information regarding MEBA school history can be found on their website, *MEBAschool.org/about-us.*

The Merchant Marine Act of 1970 was signed by Richard Nixon during the Vietnam War. This legislation was passed by Congress overwhelmingly (House 307-1, Senate 68-1) according to Lt S.W. Emery, Jr., USN, in the U.S. Naval Institute's magazine, *Proceedings*, dated March 1971. The major component of this legislation was a shift in the Construction Differential Subsidy (CDS) from 50% to 35% by 1976. Also, ships built under the CDS for operation in a specific trade must remain in that trade. Bulk carriers, both dry and liquid cargo, were added to the ships eligible for the CDS.

According to the United Nations annual report titled "Review of Maritime Transport" (1970 and 1971), during the Vietnam War, the U.S. Merchant Marine was among the largest in the world. The largest fleets between 1965 and 1970 were those of Liberia, the United Kingdom, Japan, and Norway, with the United States in fifth place. While wartime boosted shipping and employment, the postwar era saw a return to fewer ships.

In 1986, President Ronald Reagan vetoed (pocket veto) a bill authorizing funding for the Maritime Administration and the Federal Maritime Commission. He would not sign the bill because he did not believe that private industries should receive direct government assistance. Additionally, he sought to repeal the Ship Construction and Mortgage Insurance Program, commonly referred to as Title XI.

This is documented in the article "Reagan Vetoes Funding" by Robert F. Morison in the *Journal of Commerce* from October 1986. Reagan wanted to repeal all existing credit guarantee programs, not just Title XI. He apparently did not realize the value of the U.S. Merchant Marine for national security.

Despite the high mortality rate during World War II, merchant mariners were not eligible for veterans' benefits until Congress passed a law in 1988 granting benefits to those who served in specific war zones. Congress attempted to pass the "Honoring Our WWII Merchant Mariners Act of 2017," a bill providing a one-time $25,000 payment to surviving merchant mariners to compensate them for not receiving veterans' benefits until 1988. The bill failed, but it was reintroduced in 2023 and again in 2025. In 2020, merchant mariners who served during World War II were given a Congressional Gold Medal. The medal is displayed at the American Merchant Marine Museum in Kings Point, NY, and each surviving mariner received a bronze replica. It took decades to recognize and honor those who served in the most dangerous jobs during World War II.

In 1970, China was not listed in the top 10 shipping fleets in the world. By 1980, China had begun building its fleet of merchant ships. And by 2002, China had a significantly larger fleet than the United States. According to data from the United Nations Conference on Trade and Development, January 2020, the United States ranked tenth in the world for total deadweight tons of carrying capacity, with 57.2 million tons (2.79% of the world's tonnage).

By comparison, China ranked third, with 228.4 million tons (11.15% of the world's tonnage). In April 2021, Frank Holmes ranked the top ten countries with the largest shipping fleets by deadweight tonnage (*www.usfunds.com*), confirming the

U.S. in tenth place, while Greece, Japan, and China ranked first, second, and third, respectively.

In 1944, General Eisenhower said, "When final victory is ours, there is no organization that will share its credit more deservedly than the Merchant Marine." General MacArthur said, "I hold no branch higher in esteem than the merchant marine." (Find these quotes and more information at the website *centerformaritimestrategy.org* in their "What to Watch 2023" report.)

However, the United States had allowed China to surpass it in the size and scope of both the merchant fleet and the shipyards that build and repair the fleet. According to Senator Mark Kelly (a Kings Point graduate), "China has more than 5,500 merchant vessels, while the U.S. has 80 U.S.-flagged merchant ships operating worldwide." This information can be found on the website below by scrolling down to the article "Current Score: China 5500, U.S. 80," dated February 2024. (*www.wearetheusmma.com/news*)

Lori Ann LaRocco published a blog for CNBC in April 2024 titled "Biden Promise to Rival China on Shipbuilding Faces a Big Economic Problem." She reported that the Biden administration recognized that a strong merchant marine was vital to national security. And that in a prolonged war, China would have the advantage because the U.S. no longer had sufficient domestic steel and shipyards to rebuild either its Navy or its merchant fleet. His goal was to impose additional tariffs on steel imported from China and to revive the construction of merchant ships in the U.S.

However, the Reagan administration had eliminated the Construction Differential Subsidies, and the cost of U.S.-built ships in 2024 was as much as four to six times the cost of foreign ship construction. While providing subsidies for U.S. shipyards will help revitalize that industry, shipyards cannot purchase steel and increase their workforce unless they have actual orders for new ships.

On December 19, 2024, Sen. Mark Kelly (D-AZ), Sen. Todd Young (R-IN), Rep. John Garamendi (D-CA), and Rep. Trent Kelly (R-MS) introduced the bipartisan Shipbuilding and Harbor Infrastructure for Prosperity and Security (SHIPS) for America Act. The act was designed to coordinate U.S. maritime policy, expand the U.S. international fleet, enhance the competitiveness of U.S.-flagged vessels, and enlarge the shipyard industrial base. It would create a Maritime Security and Trust Fund to reinvest industry fees into maritime security programs and infrastructure. A maritime security advisor would be added to the White House staff.

The ultimate goal is to increase the U.S. international fleet by an additional 250 U.S.-built, U.S.-manned ships within 10 years. The bill considers this a national security issue, necessary to compete with China's vessels and shipbuilding capacity. More details are provided in the article "Bipartisan SHIPS for America Act introduced," dated December 2024, found at *workboat.com.*

By 2025, Kings Point was over 80 years old and was falling into disrepair, just like the merchant marine. Recognizing the importance of the ship's officers, a bipartisan bill, supported by President Trump, was passed that included $1 billion to revitalize the academy. A report by Robert Brodsky in *Newsday,* April 2025, confirmed that an estimated $54 million will be spent in the first year drawing up plans for the revitalization. Just over $107 million will then be spent each year for the next nine years to repair and upgrade the failing infrastructure.

Despite the desire to increase the number of ships built in the U.S. and the number of officers to staff them, no one knows what the future will hold for the U.S. merchant marine, and equally important, the merchant mariners who operate the ships. In an interview with MEBA Gulf Coast Vice-President Adam Smith in 2024, MEBA had approximately 2,700 members and 1,300 applicants (engineers and deck officers awaiting member status). These numbers included officers who man barges on inland waterways, ships operating on the Great Lakes and ferry boats, as well as the ocean-going vessels. The most difficult positions to fill are senior positions, such as chief engineers and first assistant engineers. At the time of this publication, the current pay range for chief engineers is $240,000 to $320,000 per year, plus benefits.

Chapter 2

Jesse Calhoon

> We will send ships and Marines as soon as possible
> for the protection of American life and property.
> PRESIDENT THEODORE ROOSEVELT

★ JESSE CALHOON WAS arguably the most influential person ever to serve as an elected official in MEBA. He was president of the union from 1963 to 1984, longer than any other president in the union's 150-year history.

Jesse Mayo Calhoon was born in Belhaven, North Carolina, on April 4, 1923. His family was a farming family that supplemented their income with fishing. In 1939, when he was 16 years old, he went to sea as a coal passer in the ship's engine room. He later joined the National Maritime Union (NMU) and worked as a fireman and later an oiler.

During World War II, Calhoon sailed in the war zone many times, including several trips on the dangerous Murmansk run, delivering supplies to the troops in Europe. He also helped move supplies on ships during the invasion of North Africa and Sicily. Fortunately, he survived when the ship he was working on was torpedoed in the Gulf of Mexico.

In 1943, Jesse graduated from the U.S. Merchant Marine Officer Candidate School in New London, Connecticut, and soon earned his third assistant engineer license. Before he was 21 years old, he joined MEBA. He continued sailing as a ship's officer during and after the war. He was sailing as chief engineer by 1949. The MEBA newsletter, *Marine Officer,* published a special report on Jesse Calhoon in the Winter 2014 publication—"Longtime President and Father of M.E.B.A. Modern History Jesse Calhoon Sails Into the Sunset."

Jesse was politically astute and, in 1954, began his ascension through the ranks as a Business Manager at the MEBA Norfolk Local 11. In 1959, he was elected National MEBA Secretary-Treasurer. Edwin Altman was elected president, but shortly after the election, Altman took a leave of absence to work on John F. Kennedy's presidential campaign, and Calhoon took over as acting MEBA President in Altman's absence.

Jesse Calhoon always had an eye for the future. When he first took office, MEBA consisted of a group of local halls that were somewhat independent. Calhoon worked to overhaul the system and create three major districts: The Atlantic and Gulf Coast District, the Pacific Coast District, and the Rivers and Great Lakes District. In 1960, the MEBA local halls voted overwhelmingly to reorganize into the three major districts.

The Brotherhood of Marine Engineers (BME) was a competing union that was chartered in 1949 as an affiliate of the Seamen's International Union (SIU), which is a union representing unlicensed seamen. The BME gained autonomy in 1953 from SIU and eventually merged with MEBA Local 101 on the Great Lakes in 1959. Once MEBA had converted the union structure from local halls to the three districts, the Great Lakes and Rivers District Executive Committee (a board of directors) drew up plans for the new district, named District 2 MEBA. (Read about this at amo-union.org/history/.)

These changes in MEBA's structure took place while Calhoon was the acting MEBA president. At a special convention in March 1963, he was officially tapped to fill Altman's expired term. Six months later, in September 1963, Calhoon was elected to a full term as national president. In December 1963, he was elected as MEBA District 1 President.

In 1968, Calhoon oversaw the merger of the coastal districts, Atlantic, Gulf, and Pacific, into a single district named District No.1-PCD, MEBA. The National MEBA (NMEBA) now represented two districts: District No.1-PCD, MEBA, and District 2 MEBA. The National MEBA remained in this format, with two competing unions operating as District 1 and District 2 for nearly twenty years. The only change in the structure was adding the Radio Operators Union (ROU) to the National MEBA as District 3. It was also during this time period that the Calhoon MEBA Engineering School graduated its first class of licensed marine engineers.

Calhoon was a visionary, but he knew talent when he saw it and supplemented his skills with experts. One such expert was Lee Pressman. Pressman was a prominent union lawyer and served as general counsel for MEBA. His first representation of MEBA occurred in 1935. In 1936, Pressman was named general counsel for the Council of Industrial Organizations (CIO) before it merged with the American Federation of Labor (AFL) and became the AFL-CIO. Pressman had communist leanings in his political beliefs and was considered by one union leader to be "the most important communist in the country," according to Wikipedia. In 1948, Pressman was fired from his position as CIO general counsel but continued to represent MEBA among other clients. In the same year, Pressman was called before the House Committee on Un-American Activities.

However, he exercised his Fifth Amendment rights and refused to answer questions regarding his membership in the Communist Party. He was called before Congress again in 1950 and did testify this time. His communist leanings damaged his law practice, and by 1951, Pressman had only one major client remaining—MEBA (*wikipedia.org*). Pressman worked with MEBA and Jesse Calhoon until Pressman's death in 1969. Together, Calhoon and Pressman made great strides in pay and benefits for the MEBA membership in the 1960s.

Jesse Calhoon was a shrewd negotiator. He used his position of strength created by the shortage of marine engineers during the Vietnam War to negotiate better pay and benefits. He was also a tough negotiator. Calhoon was infamous for kicking a shipping company executive in the head during negotiations. *60 Minutes* reported on this in its October 3, 1976, episode, "Unions, Money and Politics." Calhoon's son, Curtis Calhoon, provided details on the interview with *60 Minutes*. He explained that the company executive was being disrespectful to Calhoon during the negotiation sessions.

During a break, Calhoon approached the man and told him that if he continued, Calhoon would jump up on the table and kick him in the teeth. In the next session, the company executive continued to be disrespectful. At that point, Calhoon jumped up on the table and kicked him.

Another unconfirmed story about his negotiating tactics involved the actual signing of a contract. Calhoon had negotiated several gains, and as the company negotiator was about to sign the contract, he grumbled, "I'm surprised you didn't ask for steak every Thursday night." It is alleged that Calhoon pulled the contract from under his pen and replied, "I forgot about that!" He added that clause to the contract.

It is alleged that for years, steak was served on MEBA-contracted ships every Thursday night. (The author sailed on MEBA-contracted ships for over 20 years and ate steak every Thursday night.) Curtis Calhoon did not confirm this rumor, but he pointed out that one of his father's negotiating tactics was to feed the negotiating teams with a large buffet. He would place the buffet close to the negotiating room so one could smell the food and feel the hunger. But, he wouldn't let anyone eat until the negotiations were concluded.

Calhoon also gave preference to Calhoon MEBA Engineering School graduates whenever possible. One approach was to mandate that job applicants for automated ships must have prior experience working on such vessels. This created a Catch-22 situation. How do you get automation experience if you have to have automation experience to work on an automated ship? Automation became available around 1964 and slowly entered the fleet as ships were replaced.

One Calhoon MEBA Engineering School graduate, Alex Shandrowsky, explained in an interview with the author that while he was working as a cadet during his sea year, he was assigned to a new automated ship. After graduation, he went to the union hall and jumped over several senior union members because he had automation experience. The older members had not yet sailed on an automated ship. Eventually, the automation requirement was lifted.

Another method of giving Calhoon MEBA Engineering School graduates an advantage occurred in the early 1970s. *60 Minutes* explains in "Unions, Money and Politics" (October 1976) that Calhoon is alleged to have had a hatred for the U.S. Merchant Marine Academy and the five state maritime academies, and would close the books to academy graduates wanting to join the union. This gave Calhoon graduates an advantage: union-contracted shipping companies and taxpayer dollars funding Calhoon MEBA Engineering School.

Opponents of Calhoon's preference for Calhoon MEBA Engineering School graduates pointed out that taxpayers pay for the academies and also pay for the federal ship subsidies, which provide refunds to the shipping companies. In other words, taxpayers are paying to educate academy graduates who then cannot get jobs on union-contracted oceangoing vessels subsidized by federal dollars.

Calhoon's negotiating tactics went beyond the shipping contracts. It is reported that he spent a significant amount of time at the White House while Richard Nixon was president. The *mebaunion.org* website notes he assisted Nixon in passing the Merchant Marine Act of 1970. He also fought to prevent the export of Alaskan North Slope oil to foreign countries. An export ban was in place, and studies estimated that lifting the export ban would cost the U.S. Merchant Marine thousands of jobs. Calhoon went to Capitol Hill, using his finely honed negotiating skills, to keep the ban in place.

He also spoke before Congress in 1970 in support of H.R. 13832, a bill to construct forty LNG tankers.

Representing the AFL-CIO Maritime Committee, he stated that liquefied natural gas (LNG) ships should be constructed in U.S. shipyards and manned by U.S. merchant mariners. The benefit would be to stimulate the economy, provide better control over the construction and operation of the ships entering the U.S., and reduce the dependence on foreign sources for supplying energy. (See the transcript of Jesse Calhoon's speech before Congress on June 8, 1972, titled "Construction of Forty Liquefied Natural Gas Tankers.")

Jesse Calhoon expanded the marine engineer union to include deck officers (also known as mates). Chevron Oil had a company union, but was experiencing some difficulty operating it. They approached the International Organization of Masters, Mates and Pilots (MM&P) and asked for help. MM&P declined the offer because it involved both mates and engineers, and MM&P was strictly a deck officers' union. Calhoon saw this as an opportunity to expand the union and brought the Chevron union members into MEBA.

This proved to be a brilliant move. In the late 1970s, two shipping companies, Energy Transportation Corporation and El Paso LNG, entered the LNG transportation business. The ships were unique and required a unique contract. The ships were very sophisticated and required the best officers. Calhoon negotiated with the shipping companies to supply both deck officers and engineers and gave the shipping companies the *right of selection*. The shipping companies could hire and fire any ship's officer as long as the replacement officer was a member of MEBA.

The companies also had control over officer promotions and usually promoted from within rather than accept a new man from the hiring hall. Calhoon agreed to a *no-strike clause* because the contracts between the shipping companies and the LNG receiving terminals had stringent schedules, and ships couldn't be delayed. In exchange for the no-strike clause, Calhoon negotiated a deal that, when an agreement was finally reached for contract renewal, the agreement would be retroactive. If negotiation took a while, the ships' officers would receive a check for any pay increases retroactive to the end of the previous contract.

During his tenure in office, Calhoon acquired several large real estate assets for use by the union. The MEBA national headquarters were located in Manhattan for many years, because many of the U.S. shipping companies were located there. In 1976, Calhoon negotiated the purchase of the multi-story building at 444 North Capitol Street in Washington, D.C., for $30 million. Calhoon saw the value of being close to Congress and 1600 Pennsylvania Avenue, literally.

According to his son, Curtis Calhoon, Jesse Calhoon had the opportunity to purchase the property but had to move quickly to close the deal. Usually, he would need to have the purchase approved by the Benefit Plans Trustees, because he was purchasing the building as an investment for the Benefit Plans. Instead, he bought the building and then attended the trustee meeting, where he informed them of his actions.

It was a situation where he had violated the protocol, but by doing so, he had acquired an outstanding asset for the Benefit Plans. Calhoon's office on the eighth floor had a wall of windows overlooking the Capitol Dome. One union member went to the Washington headquarters to do some volunteer work. When he saw Calhoon's office, he commented on the opulence. Calhoon responded, "If I can't negotiate my own contract, I have no business negotiating yours."

Under Calhoon's leadership, MEBA made substantial donations to political candidates, which gave him a great deal of clout in Congress and the Whitehouse. In 1976, when Jimmy Carter was running for president, Calhoon met with Carter and decided to support him in his presidential campaign. It was reported that twenty-five MEBA members, their spouses, and a few executives from the shipping company donated $25,000 to the Carter campaign in a single day—$1,000 each.

Nine days later, Calhoon sponsored a fundraiser for Carter. Union and shipping company attendees each donated $1,000 to hear him speak. The Carter campaign raised $150,000 in one night, according to a *60 Minutes* report, "Unions, Money and Politics" (October 1976). Keep in mind, this was 1976. The U.S. Census report from 1978 notes that the median family income was only $14,960, showing that $1,000 was upwards of a month's wages for the average American.

Carter was not the only candidate to receive contributions. Over a dozen Congressmen and Senators received substantial contributions from MEBA. In exchange, when Calhoon spoke, Congress listened. Calhoon also held a few government advisory positions over the years and took part in the Maritime Advisory Committee established by the Secretary of Transportation and the President's Export Council, which gave him access to the White House. Calhoon was an officer of the Joint Maritime Congress, which monitored maritime legislation in Congress.

By 1978, the MEBA pension fund was close to fully funded and exceptionally well-managed. In the next union contract, Calhoon negotiated that the contracted companies would no longer need to contribute to the pension plan.

Instead, on June 16, 1978, the MEBA Money Purchase Benefit was started. The Money Purchase Benefit (MPB) was a program in which contracted companies made contributions into an individual account in the name of the employed union member, rather than into a general fund. When an officer joined a ship, an amount equal to five percent of the officer's base wage was paid into the individual's MPB account. Now, MEBA members had not only a pension plan but also an MPB account when they retired, according to the Summary Plan Description of the MEBA Pension Trust Money Purchase Benefit Plan (May 2022).

During his tenure, Calhoon established a self-funded medical benefit that paid 100% of medical costs and offered a free annual diagnostic physical (including travel expenses) to any members and their families who wished to participate. Pensioners were also eligible for the annual diagnostic physical. The diagnostic physical often identified severe conditions, like cancer or diabetes, before the member had any idea there was a problem. The annual diagnostic physical was available to all union members, but was mandatory for continued employment with a few contracted companies.

The potential disadvantage of the medical benefit was that members were covered only while they were employed, including vacation time. Ninety days after a member's vacation ran out, he was no longer eligible for medical benefits until he returned to work. This occurred because the contracted companies paid on a per-man-per-day basis. If a member was not working, payments were not being made into the medical benefits plan on his behalf.

In the mid-1970s, MEBA purchased a 656-acre property just outside of Easton, Maryland, on the eastern shore of the Chesapeake Bay. According to the MEBA website, the property consisted of two estates, Kirkland Hall and Perry Hall, which had later become the now-defunct Kirkland Hall Junior College (*www.MEBASchool.org/About-us/School-History*). Initially, the property was used for lifeboat and sea survival classes; however, starting in 1979, the property was updated, and additional buildings were constructed. The Calhoon MEBA Engineering School relocated from its original location on Light Street in downtown Baltimore to the beautiful estates on the Chesapeake Bay in the early 1980s.

When people didn't listen to Calhoon, they often paid the price. In 1981, during the Reagan administration, the Professional Air Traffic Controllers Organization (PATCO) sought to go on strike for better pay and shorter working hours due to job-related stress. PATCO was a union affiliated with MEBA, and Calhoon strongly advised PATCO President Robert Poli against striking because negotiations are most effective when conducted from a position of strength, and this was not the time.

PATCO ignored his advice and still went on strike. Reagan responded by firing every air traffic controller who hadn't returned to work. Reagan based his decision on the federal law from 1955 that prevents government employees from going on strike. Additionally, PATCO was terminated as a union in 1981.

Union affiliation is necessary for newer unions. When the AFL and CIO merged into the AFL-CIO, unions that belonged to either organization became charter members. The AFL-CIO closed its books to new members, and the only way for a newly formed union to become part of the organization was to become affiliated with a charter member. An example is PATCO, the air traffic controller union founded in 1968. Air traffic controllers were not unionized in 1955 when the AFL-CIO was established because air traffic was still in its infancy. When they organized PATCO, they did so as an affiliate of MEBA. In addition, MEBA established the Federation of Public Employees (FOPE), a union in Florida consisting of public employees, such as law enforcement and school workers, which became a division of MEBA District 1.

Calhoon was very protective of MEBA's image. One of the female employees in the Washington, D.C. office was featured posing nude in "Girls of Washington" in *Playboy* magazine. Calhoon was not pleased, and he responded by having the nude photo blown up to poster size and framed. Then, he hung the photo above the employee's desk. The young lady quit the next day.

With all of Calhoon's success, he did have one failure. The pension plan funded the construction and operation of two ships under his administration, and he served as the director of the shipping company, First American Bulk Carrier. A lawsuit was filed in December 1985, after he had retired, which challenged the pension plan's ownership of a shipping company as a violation of ERISA, the federal law governing pensions. The courts ruled in July 1986 that the pension plan must divest itself of any interest in First American Bulk Carrier, according to the U.S. District Court for the District of Columbia, Civil Action No. 85-3896.

By the end of his presidency, Jesse Calhoon had created a well-structured union. At the top of the union was the National MEBA. The National MEBA had three districts: MEBA District 1, MEBA District 2, and MEBA District 3. All three districts had a board of directors, called a District Executive Committee (DEC). Elections would be held in MEBA District 1 every three years. At that time, the President, Atlantic Coast Vice President, Gulf Coast Vice President, Pacific Coast Vice President, and Secretary/Treasurer were elected.

In the same election, union members would vote for convention delegates. The convention delegates from all three districts would meet at a National Convention the following year. They would vote for the National MEBA President and other officials who would make up the National Executive Committee (NEC).

Election of the NMEBA officials and NEC members by the convention delegates was similar to the election of the President of the United States by the Electoral College. Just as each state sent delegates to the Electoral College, where they have the final vote for the President of the United States, each district sent delegates to the National Convention. The delegates had the final vote for the National MEBA Officials and NEC members.

District 1 was able to control NMEBA through the convention delegates because Calhoon had established rules where the number of delegates representing each district was based on the amount of dues paid to the union, not the number of members in the union. Members of District 1 were the highest paid and, therefore, paid the highest dues. This skewed the number of convention delegates in favor of District 1, and Jesse Calhoon was not only the District 1 President but also elected National MEBA President throughout his tenure.

Jesse Calhoon did things throughout his presidency that were not always completely honest, but whatever he did always benefited the members of MEBA District 1. Some considered him a benevolent dictator because his actions, whether questionable or not, consistently generated more money and benefits for the membership.

Over time, most union members became somewhat complacent; whatever Calhoon wanted was okay with them. The complacency extended into the election process. Mail-in ballots were used for voting because half of the membership was on ships spread across the world, and the other half was on vacation, spread across the country. The branch agents and patrolmen in the halls across the country would ask members to turn over their blank or nearly blank ballots.

Houston Branch Agent Claude W. "Bill" Daulley would instruct a member to fill out the ballot for people they knew and wanted. However, if they didn't know everyone running for positions in other ports, they should return the incomplete ballot to him. Daulley would then fill in the blanks and even mail it on behalf of the member. It should be noted that he asked this author for his ballot on multiple occasions.

The members who turned over their ballots to the union officials would not know who they had voted for or if the ballot had even been mailed. If the member voted for someone the incumbent officials didn't want, the ballot would just disappear. Accepting unsealed ballots was illegal, yet the members continued to receive more money and benefits. As a result, only a few activists would complain, and they were a minority. Complacency and apathy ruled.

Chapter 3

Along Came DeFries

> *The maintenance of a merchant marine*
> *is of the utmost importance for national defense*
> *and the service of our commerce.*
> PRESIDENT CALVIN COOLIDGE

★ A MAJOR EVENT was the retirement of Jesse Calhoon at the end of 1984, after nearly forty years in the union and 22 years as president. At a trustee meeting for MEBA Benefit Plans held at the Biltmore Hotel in Colorado Springs, Colorado, he faced an unprecedented challenge as president when other union trustees, with Executive Vice President C.E. "Gene" DeFries at the helm, voted against him on various benefit matters like medical and pension plans. Jesse saw the writing on the wall; he no longer had the control he had enjoyed for over 20 years, and decided it was time to retire, according to an interview with his son, Curtis Calhoon.

In the 1984 elections, Gene DeFries ran as Calhoon's successor and won the election. C.W. "Bill" Daulley, the Houston branch agent, was elected as Gulf Coast Vice President and branch agent for New Orleans. Alexander "Doc" Cullison was elected branch agent for the Houston Hall, replacing Bill Daulley.

Gene DeFries took the reins in January 1985. He believed that a new direction was necessary to maintain the high standards of MEBA and possibly rebuild the U.S. Merchant Marine. As things were, union members were experiencing a battle between labor and the shipping companies, which were promoting the idea that the only way to gain (or maintain) jobs was through reduced wages and benefits. DeFries decided to take a bold step and merge the MEBA with an unlicensed union, the National Maritime Union (NMU).

The U.S. Coast Guard licensed the officers, while the crew was documented by the Coast Guard but not licensed. Merging the two unions would be beneficial in many ways. The combined unions would be able to present a single contract for manning ships that would include the deck officers, engineers, and the unlicensed crew, all under one umbrella. The shipping industry was on a downward curve, and standing united with a single contract would theoretically give the merged union additional bargaining power.

In addition to improved negotiating strength, the unions would also combine their infrastructures, moving union halls into one location in each port and bringing their administrations under one roof. They would be able to eliminate redundancy in their respective administrations. All of this was intended to reduce costs and, at the same time, create a lean, mean maritime union to go up against the shipping companies, who, at this particular time, had the advantage. One disadvantage of this plan was that MEBA District 2 was still a competing union offering contracts with lower pay and fewer benefits.

In March 1987, MEBA District 1 and NMU began discussing a possible merger. The NMU put the concept to a vote and received overwhelming support in favor of a merger. The *NMU Pilot*, published in April 1988, reported that the NMU voted for the actual merger at the end of 1987, and the merger passed with a vote of 4788 to 417 (over 11 to 1).

MEBA members weren't as thrilled as NMU members about the merger. The plan to merge the licensed and unlicensed unions had one major drawback: the MEBA Pension Plan was fully funded, whereas the unlicensed pension was not as solvent. As of December 1986, the MEBA had just under 4,000 members, and the pension was fully funded, with a little less than $900,000,000 in the pension plan.

By comparison, the NMU had just under 7500 members and about $300,000,000 in its pension plan. Based on the "Actuarial Valuation and Review" from September 1987 by Martin E. Segal Company, the NMU pension met the minimum federal requirements for a pension plan. The unlicensed workers thought the merger was a great idea because their union was slowly losing members and jobs. However, the licensed officers were against it, as merging the pensions would almost certainly eliminate the fully funded status of their pension and leave them with a less stable pension plan.

DeFries and the union leadership began a campaign promising that the pensions would be kept separate and never merged. It took several months of visiting the ships and attending union meetings to convince the membership that the merger was a good idea. Danny Colon, a patrolman based at the New York hall, was sent to Japan to sell the merger to the ETC fleet. A group of officers expressed concern about the pension, and Colon assured them that the pension was safe. When he returned to New York, he sent some of the officers a personal letter with the *Marine Journal Special Merger Supplement* enclosed. The *Marine Journal* was a union newspaper that kept the membership informed about union news. The supplement urged support for the merger.

Reluctantly, the licensed officers voted to merge the two unions with the assurance that the MEBA Pension Plan would be protected and never merged with the Unlicensed Division Pension Plan. The union would conduct and conclude the vote before April 1, 1988—April Fool's Day. The *NMU Pilot* from April 1988 reported that the MEBA approved the merger with a vote of 2244 to 495 (less than 5:1).

With the merger approved by both unions, MEBA District 1 and NMU replaced District 1 under the NMEBA umbrella as MEBA/NMU. The new district was divided into two divisions: the Licensed Division and the Unlicensed Division. Officials of both divisions were appointed, not elected, until the next election cycle. The newly appointed officials of MEBA/NMU were:

- President—C.E. "Gene" DeFries (former MEBA President)
- Executive Vice President—Shannon J. Wall (former NMU President)
- Secretary—Louis Parise (former NMU Secretary/Treasurer)
- Treasurer—Clyde E. Dodson (former MEBA Executive Vice President)

- Vice President, Licensed Division—R.F. Schamann (former MEBA Vice President)
- Vice President, Unlicensed Division—Rene Lioeanjie (former NMU Vice President)

The newly appointed officials of the Licensed Division were:

- Chairman—C.E. "Gene" DeFries (former MEBA President)
- Vice Chairman—Clyde E. Dodson (former MEBA Executive Vice President)
- Directors—C.W. Daulley (former MEBA Vice President)
- R.F. Schamann (former MEBA Vice President)
- Karl M. Landgrebe (former MEBA Secretary/Treasurer)

The newly appointed officials of the Unlicensed Division were:

- Chairman—Shannon J. Wall (former NMU President)
- Vice Chairman—Louis Parise (former NMU Secretary/Treasurer)
- Directors—Rene Lioeanjie (former NMU Vice President)
- James Paterson (former NMU Vice President)
- Elwood Hampton (former NMU Vice President)

Gene DeFries had a larger plan than just merging the MEBA and the NMU. Three months after the MEBA/NMU merger, he began once again investigating a possible merger of the newly formed MEBA/NMU with MEBA District 2 to form one massive union of mates, engineers, and unlicensed crew. This would vastly increase his ability to negotiate with contracted companies, rather than competing with MEBA District 2 for contracts. Of course, DeFries planned to be in charge of it all.

He presented a proposal to District 2 a few months after his successful merger with the NMU. However, the plan was rejected, and MEBA District 2 continued to compete for contracts with MEBA District 1. MEBA District 2 was already affiliated, but not merged, with the unlicensed Seamen's International Union (SIU), and merging with the MEBA/NMU would create problems in their relationship with the SIU. This information was documented in the memorandum dated July 20, 1988, "Merger with D-2, AMO."

For years, the MEBA contracts have had a clause for severance pay if a contracted vessel was transferred from the U.S. flag to a foreign registry. The primary reason for transferring a ship to a foreign registry, also known as a "flag of convenience," was to hire foreign crews at significantly lower wages and, as a bonus, avoid the stringent requirements of the U.S. Coast Guard. If a ship moved to a foreign registry and MEBA officers were replaced, the company had to pay them, as per the severance clause, one month's pay per year of service on that ship, up to twelve months.

In February 1988, just before the merger of MEBA and NMU, Gene DeFries sent a proposed resolution to all DEC members. The resolution defined *termination* of employment with the district to include "consolidation, merger, or other combination of District 1 with another union resulting in the substantial reorganization of District No.1." The next day, the DEC passed the resolution by telephone vote and ratified it the day after that, according to the Memorandum, "Report on Independent Investigation of Severance Payments to Union Officials," March 1990.

One month later, on March 17, 1988, the Severance Pay Committee certified a total of nearly $2 million in severance pay to five members of the DEC. A short time later, they added Karl Landgrebe, which pushed the total to $2,014,061. (This can be verified through the U.S. District Court for the District of Maryland, Civil Action No. S-90-822.) Individual severance pay was as follows:

- C.E. "Gene" DeFries $936,593
- Clyde Dodson $396,187
- C.W. "Bill" Daulley $134,651
- R.F. Schamann $270,699
- Donald Masingo $249,000
- Karl Landgrebe $ 26,931

The DEC officials were receiving a severance package as a result of being terminated as union officials in MEBA District 1. None of these union officials actually lost their jobs. They remained in the same office, at the same desk, and in the same general position with essentially the same pay; the only thing that changed was the letterhead. It was no longer called MEBA District 1; now it was called MEBA/NMU.

Throughout the entire process, the membership was never notified of the new severance plan. The membership only learned about the severance pay when it was reported in a trade magazine, the *Journal of Commerce*. DeFries had taken steps to conceal the severance payments from the membership, specifically by failing to include them in the minutes for the meeting where the severance package was approved and then directing the union's controller not to reveal any details of the plan.

The MEBA District 1 Bylaws allowed the DEC to establish compensation levels for officers and employees; however, it also stated, "unless otherwise directed by a majority vote of the membership." When the membership finally discovered the severance payments, which amounted to approximately half of the union's $4 million working capital, a group of union members filed a lawsuit to recover the money.

Severance pay was not the only merger-related issue that concerned the membership. A story spread through the union that someone working on a ship had retired recently. The ship he was working on threw a retirement party, which was common; however, a few months later, he was back at work on his old job on the ship.

How could a man retire and then return to his old job? When he went to apply for his retirement, the secretary in the Pension Benefits office informed him that he qualified under a new retirement rule and could take his retirement as a lump sum while continuing to work. It appeared that the District Executive Committee (DEC), with Gene DeFries as chairman, established a new rule, known as the "Alternative Lump Sum Buyout Rule," which allowed certain individuals meeting specific criteria to retire while continuing to work. They would get a one-time payment, a lump sum, instead of a monthly pension check, and they could continue to work in their current position in the union.

The DEC had written a very restrictive set of criteria to qualify for the Alternative Lump Sum Buyout. Under the new criteria, *all* DEC members were eligible to retire and continue working; however, the rule was not so stringent that no one else qualified, resulting in about 2% of the general union membership also qualifying. That's how the members found out—from the two percent! Why would the DEC do this? The reason was apparent: they planned to merge the pensions, and they wanted to ensure they received their money before the fully funded pension was destroyed.

The members later discovered that while MEBA union officials were promising not to merge the pensions, the NMU leadership was assuring its members that they *would, in fact,* merge the pensions. In the April 1988 edition of the *NMU Pilot*, NMU President Shannon Wall wrote a multi-page article about the merger of MEBA and NMU. In it, he wrote, "The next step along the road to total merger is the merger of our collectively bargained Pension, Welfare, Vacation, and Training Plans."

The NMU Trustees Meeting, June 24, 1987, adopted the following resolution: The *Now Therefore* portion of the resolution stated, "Be it resolved that this Board of Trustees hereby approves, in principle, the merger of said plans upon such terms and conditions as are approved by the Boards of Trustees of said plans and subject to all applicable laws." Note that this occurred in June 1987, months before either union had voted for the merger.

Clearly, Gene DeFries had planned to merge the pensions all along. Less than six months after the merger vote, the MEBA/NMU's Park Avenue lawyers filed a formal pension merger document dated August 29, 1988. The document, titled "Merger of MEBA Pension Trust and NMU Pension Trust," was filed with the Pension Benefit Guarantee Corporation (PBGC), which was based in Washington, DC, and monitored pension mergers.

How were they able to make these new rules, and how could the membership stop them? As it turns out, when the membership voted for the merger, the "Agreement of Merger" had a clause which stated, "The District Executive Committee shall direct the administration of all District affairs, properties, policies, and personnel in any and all areas, including those not otherwise specifically provided for in this constitution. The District Executive Committee shall have such powers, duties, and authority as are conferred upon it by the National Constitution."

A second clause gave the District Executive Committee the power to merge the pensions: "The District Executive Committee will initiate whatever steps are necessary to commence the process of merging all benefits plans covering the members and officers of both NMU and District 1-PCD, MEBA..." In short, the new constitution and bylaws resulting from the merger gave the DEC increased power while simultaneously limiting the power of the licensed membership. According to the magazine *Soundings*, an article in their January 1991 issue titled "Incumbents Fight Back" reports that under the new MEBA/NMU Constitution, the DEC now had the power to:

- Develop and direct the union's policy and business between conventions.
- Interpret the constitution itself.
- Submit to a referendum vote any issue, policy, or action.
- Convene a special convention with all the powers of regular conventions.
- Modify or alter the rules governing those conventions.
- Remove any delegate deemed disorderly or disruptive.
- Rule on any challenge to the conduct of elections for union officers.
- Open or close any port offices and branches of either division and reassign or lay off their branch agents.

It would appear that the new leadership wanted an authoritarian DEC and used the merger to move in that direction. While the union leadership made all the documents available to the members, most members were complacent. They listened to the leadership, accepting what they were told as complete and factual, rather than reading the fine print in the revised MEBA/NMU Constitution and Bylaws.

The truth was that the information provided to members was neither complete nor factual. The members had been given a single vote of *yes* or *no* on the entire merger package, and by voting *yes*, the membership was also allowing the DEC to strengthen its control of the union.

What were they going to do now? The majority of MEBA members had voted for the merger, or had they? More than once, branch agents and patrolmen in the union halls had asked members for their ballots, stating that they would fill in the blanks with the candidates that would do the most good. But, the most good for whom? The complacent membership was about to find out!

Chapter 4

Time to Get MAD

> *Life is like the ocean. Waves will try to knock you down and push you back to where you started. But once you fight through them, the entire ocean is yours.*
> WWW.MAX-GROUPS.COM

★ WHEN JESSE CALHOON was the president, the membership had generally been complacent. They knew that the leadership was requesting ballots and suspected that they were almost certainly stacking the deck in their favor. This didn't matter because the pay was increasing steadily, and the benefits were fantastic, so why would anyone complain? Calhoon could do whatever he wanted.

The union leadership also preferred a complacent membership. However, among all the complacent members, there were always a few dissenters who wanted the elections to be honest and wanted a wiser use of union funds. They would question everything that didn't make sense to them or anything that seemed dishonest.

Apparently, the Gulf Coast union halls were more easygoing than on the East and West Coasts. In Houston, members could speak up at union meetings if they disagreed with the leadership and not be subject to blatant bullying; however, things were different in other halls. In the Baltimore Hall, with Don Masingo as the branch agent, dissenters were frequently told to "Sit down and shut up. Just vote *yes*." The branch agent was pushing *his* agenda regardless of what the membership wanted. The leadership was doing a great job and didn't want the members questioning its methods.

Elections were held every three years, during which the union would vote for the election of officers. The incumbent officers were able to run for re-election with no term limits. Things were going well, and the complacent outnumbered the dissenters, so the incumbents always won. Of course, the merger of the MEBA and NMU was also put to a union-wide vote, because it was a complete restructuring of the union, and the results would probably be the same.

Some of the more vocal members noticed that, unlike other types of elections, whenever a vote was held, the spread between those in favor and those against was consistently about the same, typically 4 to 1 in favor of the incumbents. By asking for the ballots, the union leadership could ensure that they always won by a comfortable margin. The MEBA/NMU merger was approved by a margin of 4.5 to 1.

As mentioned earlier, when Bill Daulley was the Houston branch agent, he would ask for ballots. Still, he never pressured the members to vote. This was not always the case in the other union halls. One member was shipping out of the New York hall, which was actually located in Jersey City, NJ (much like the NY Giants have their MetLife Stadium in East Rutherford, NJ). Danny Colon, a patrolman in New York, had pressured the member for his ballot when they were voting for the merger. This action was not an uncommon form of bullying. He agreed at the time, so Colon would leave him alone, but later mailed his ballot instead. According to an affidavit signed by John F. Whiteley dated June 21, 1990, he voted against the merger.

After the MEBA/NMU merger election and the subsequent start to the merging of pensions, a few of the members who were considered instigators by the leadership (and activists by the membership) got together and discussed how they could stop the merger. Alex Shandrowsky, a chief engineer and one of the activists, had asked about merging the pensions several times before the merger vote and was assured by the branch agent that the administration of both pension plans would be handled by a combined MEBA/NMU pension office, but the actual pension accounts would absolutely remain separate. Clearly, they had lied to him.

He got together with another activist, Joel Bem, a chief engineer with Sealand, currently sailing as chief engineer aboard the SL *Atlantic*. Besides being a chief engineer, Bem had also been an instructor at Calhoon MEBA Engineering School and had been head of the Engineering Department. Bem became instrumental in the fight because, besides being a former instructor and a chief engineer, he graduated magna cum laude from the U.S. Merchant Marine Academy, had a master's degree in Management Science from Johns Hopkins University, had a law degree from the University of Maryland Law School, and was a member of the Maryland Bar.

Shandrowsky and Bem discussed how to stop the pension merger. The only way to do it would be to organize an opposition group. Shandrowsky knew Don McLendon, a chief engineer with Energy Transportation Corporation (ETC). They knew each other well because they had shipped out of the same hall for years and had worked together aboard a ship, so they trusted each other.

One day, Gordon Ward knocked on Don McLendon's door. Ward lived in the Baltimore area and was hearing about the other activists. He eventually linked with Bem, Shandrowsky, and McLendon. Ward graduated from Maine Maritime Academy at the top of his class and had also been an instructor at Calhoon MEBA Engineering School. He was currently a chief engineer on the SS *Puerto Rico* for Puerto Rico Marine Management, Inc. (PRIMMI).

The group of activists was growing. The next step was meetings with like-minded members who wanted to salvage the pension and were willing to fight for it. They began having meetings at members' homes in the Baltimore area, and the group grew from four to a dozen very quickly. It was at a meeting in Don McLendon's home that Joel Bem came up with a name for the newly formed group, The MAD Committee. Initially, MAD stood for Members Against DeFries, but later stood for Members Advocating Democracy.

Dan McWiggins, in *Building Up Steam: Why the M.E.B.A. got M.AD.*, published in November 1993, explained that during the same time frame, an opposition group was also forming on the West Coast. A group calling itself *On Watch* formed in San Francisco, led by Harold Thore. Bill Langley, also a former instructor at the Calhoon MEBA Engineering School and currently a chief engineer with ETC, was an active participant in *On Watch* in the San Francisco area. William

Austin was the former labor relations instructor at Calhoon MEBA Engineering School, and his son, Mark Austin, became active with *On Watch*. Mark Austin worked out of the Seattle Hall, as did another activist, Louie Coulson.

MEBA was not the only source of activism. Walter Brown was president of FOPE. Browne was dissatisfied with the way DeFries controlled the FOPE leadership and wanted to regain control of his union. He was organizing against DeFries, not because of the merger but because DeFries ruled the FOPE with an iron fist and did not allow the members to vote for their own leadership. FOPE called their opposition group *Freeze DeFries*. Eventually, both *On Watch* and *Freeze DeFries* joined forces with the MAD Committee, and MAD became the common name.

Baltimore was the center of activity, but other key players were contacted. Ward contacted Larry O'Toole to discuss the situation. Ward and O'Toole had lived in the same town while they were both instructors at the Calhoon MEBA Engineering School and remained close friends. O'Toole was a Kings Point graduate with a master's degree in education and was currently sailing as chief engineer on the LNG Virgo with ETC. However, he was now living in Connecticut, so Ward was his connection to the fight. O'Toole lived close to Capt. Ed Carr, also in Connecticut, and Capt. Carr would eventually become an activist, helping O'Toole with the communication system to the membership.

The dissatisfaction with the merger was not limited to MEBA. Albert S. Jackson, Jr. was a member of NMU and was also against the merger. In March 1989, he filed a lawsuit demanding that the merger be nullified. His lawsuit was based on two major factors: a) he was against the NMU demanding one *yes* or *no* vote for the entire merger package, including the revised constitution and bylaws, and b) the merger package appointed all the new leadership rather than presenting an opportunity to vote them in. The NMU had not had an election of officers since 1983, and the merger would extend that past five years. His lawsuit would later become a significant piece in the fight to reverse the merger.

The union was spread across the nation, and at any given time, half of the union members were on ships sailing around the world. How do you provide information to such a widespread group of people? Today, we all have smartphones with access to the Internet, email, social media, and more. The world is very small now, but back then, communication technology was extremely limited.

The movie *Die Hard 2* (1990) took place at an airport. John McClain (Bruce Willis) uncovered an ongoing terrorist plot while waiting for his wife to land. He needed to fax a document to the police station, but had to ask an airport employee to show him how to use a fax machine, the newest form of communication technology in 1990. Remember, the merger occurred in 1988, and the conflict began in 1989. In 1989, email did not exist. The Internet was limited to universities. There was no Google, Yahoo, or Bing.

There was no Microsoft Windows; computers used DOS (Disk Operating System), and you had to have a basic knowledge of DOS to use a computer. The IBM AT was an advanced computer that was first introduced in August 1984 at a price of $4,000 to $6,000 (the price of a small car). It came with a 16-bit microprocessor, 512 KB of RAM, and a 20 MB hard drive. You could use only one program at a time; computer technology was in its infancy.

The opposition group would have to find a way to inform the general membership without the benefit of technology. Instead, they would rely on a theory called Six Degrees of Separation to get the word out. The theory states that anyone in the world can connect to anyone else in the world through six connections. Over time, this theory has morphed into a game called Six Degrees of Kevin Bacon.

Here's how it worked: You had a friend or relative named Lauretta Murphy (first degree). She co-starred in a movie called *Fatal Games* with Sally Kirkland (second degree), who was in a film called *Bruce Almighty* with Steve Carell (third degree). He, in turn, starred with Kevin Bacon in *Stupid, Crazy Love* (fourth degree).

The MAD Committee would need to rely on the same sort of interconnection, as union members were scattered on ships around the world. Most came to the union halls only for work and to attend an occasional union meeting. Interestingly, the opposition group initially turned to those they had worked with in the past or were currently working with. They knew and trusted each other and had connections across the industry; they formed the first degree of separation to spread the word.

Being former instructors, Gordon Ward, Joel Bem, Larry O'Toole, and Bill Langley connected not only with people they sailed with but also with people they had taught at the school. The instructors became the next degree of separation.

Besides needing to reach the membership, they also needed a well-crafted message. They turned to retired president

Jesse Calhoon for advice and mentorship. The MEBA Pension Plan was the hallmark of his 22 years as MEBA president. Calhoon was not pleased with the direction the union was taking after a lifetime of work, and he was unhappy that Gene DeFries had pushed him into retirement. He was willing to mentor the MAD Committee members and return the union to its former glory. Everyone knew who Jesse Calhoon was, and he became another degree of separation.

The MEBA was a small group of ships' officers, and initially, the MAD Committee would get the word out through members talking to members; however, the incumbents had major advantages. Gene DeFries and his cohorts controlled the union halls. C.W. "Bill" Daulley, as the branch agent for New Orleans, now held a vice president's position in the union, which included a seat on the DEC. By moving to New Orleans, Daulley enjoyed a significant increase in power. Daulley was replaced by Alexander "Doc" Cullison in the Houston Hall, and Doc was moving up and becoming more powerful, as well.

These men were beholden to DeFries, and as a result, the halls were not available for open discussion of issues regarding the merger. When it did come up for discussion, the branch agents would use their leadership positions to put a positive spin on the merger and the status of the pension plans. The MAD Committee would need to hold meetings somewhere else to inform the membership about what was really happening with the merger and the pension plan.

The union also issued a bi-monthly newspaper called the *Marine Journal* that provided union news and updates. Since it was controlled by the DEC, they would publish whatever they needed to guide (or misguide) the membership. The information provided in the journal was generally accurate but not necessarily complete. They never reported the severance pay for the members of the DEC. They never reported anything about plans to merge the pension, even though the DEC was actually filing paperwork necessary to do so. They never reported the Alternative Lump Sum Buyout.

To counter this biased reporting in the *Marine Journal*, the MAD Committee began publishing the *MAD Journal* in 1990, with Larry O'Toole as the editor. The purpose of the *MAD Journal* was to provide the union membership with information about the union that was not being published in the *Marine Journal*.

The MAD Committee needed working capital. They needed money, and lots of it, to pay for printing and mailing information to the membership, among other things. Email was not available until the mid-1990s, and a single mailing through the post office would cost thousands of dollars. Don McLendon assumed the position of treasurer and started by sending out a letter to the membership explaining the upcoming fight and asking for contributions. He set up a post office box in the small, somewhat remote town of Glendon, Maryland.

The union leadership did not sit idly by and watch the MAD Committee create an opposition movement against the incumbents. Intimidation was included in the counteroffensive. In an interview with Don McLendon, he stated that he would often look out his window at home and see an ominous black vehicle sitting across the street. Don also found out that a black vehicle was dumping large amounts of mail into the letter box outside the Glendon Post Office. Seeing the Glendon postmark on mail containing union information could provide some confusion. Members might think that the mail actually being sent by the union leadership via Glendon was from the MAD Committee. Informing the membership about the merging of pensions was not going to be easy or cheap.

McLendon wanted to spread the word on the East Coast and traveled from Baltimore to the New York union hall. The leadership knew about him, and he was met at the door by a union official who asked to see his union book—a small wallet-sized book that showed his dues were current. No one ever asks to see your book at a union meeting, so Don hadn't brought it with him to the New York meeting. He was denied access to the New York Hall until he could produce his union book and prove he was a member in good standing. Don called his wife and instructed her to utilize the new technology, a fax machine, and fax the page in the union book proving his dues were current. She got it to him just in time, and he was admitted to the union meeting.

Another factor in the fight to save the pension was that, while the members of the MAD Committee were outstanding engineers and highly educated, they had never run a union and faced a steep learning curve. Most people have jobs and are good at what they do, but how many people who work for a company could step into the CEO's position and immediately run the company smoothly? They were a dog chasing a car; what will the dog do if he catches it?

Then, Larry O'Toole remembered that in 1972, when he was an instructor at the Calhoon MEBA Engineering School, he had read a newspaper article written by Herman Benson, who founded the Association for Union Democracy (AUD). The AUD provided information to all types of union members around the country concerning union democracy and the members' rights in a union. The AUD was the response to the "sit-down-and-shut-up-and-just-vote-yes" philosophy of the union leadership.

Larry had saved the article for 18 years. When he found it again, he called the New York information operator (remember telephone operators?) and was pleased to find that the AUD was still in operation. He obtained the phone number for AUD in Brooklyn. When he called, he was delighted to find out that Herman Benson was still working there and was familiar with the MEBA and maritime unions. Benson was willing to help.

According to an interview with Larry O'Toole, O'Toole drove from his farm in Connecticut to Brooklyn, New York, and met with Benson. He was a man with a mission; he wanted to spread democracy throughout all unions. They discussed the situation with the MEBA/NMU and the MAD Committee. He gave O'Toole a pamphlet titled *How to Get an Honest Union Election* that contained information on the rights all union members had. The pamphlet was filled with helpful information.

The MAD Committee learned that union elections were covered by federal law under the U.S. Department of Labor. Specifically, this set of laws was called the *Labor Management Reporting and Disclosure Act (LMRDA)*, and literature published with it was helpful in union elections. LMRDA required that all unions vote by secret ballot; any ballot that is not provided in secret, such as one handed over to a branch agent or patrolman, was invalid. They learned that union members had the legal right to criticize union leadership and publish newsletters openly. Union leaders could send literature during *normal* times, but not during an *election* period. During an election period, if one candidate (the incumbent) was given a mailing list, the union was required to provide the same mailing list to all candidates.

The law mandated that the union was also required to mail campaign literature for any candidate who requested it, but at the candidate's expense. The candidate could request mailing receipts and demand to see union bills for past mailings for comparison purposes. The candidate could also ask to be present at the actual mailings to ensure their literature is mailed. The union could not censor the content of the mailings.

While most complaints must go through the Department of Labor, the LMRDA allowed for private lawsuits if the literature is not mailed. Candidates were also all given equal time in union speeches and publications, and the union could not provide resources to elect any candidate.

The union members also had the right to know how many ballots were printed and how many of those ballots were actually mailed. If too many ballots were printed, what happened to the surplus ballots? If too few ballots were mailed, where were the unmailed ballots? All the ballots, even the blank ones, needed to be accounted for.

LMRDA allowed an outside agency to monitor the election process with observers when the ballots were mailed out, when they were counted on election night, and where ballots were received and stored until Election Day. The question was: Who selects the monitoring agency? One of the most significant facts that the MAD Committee learned from the AUD was that the candidates could also select their own representatives to be present at all the above key election processes.

Since MEBA members were scattered around the country and the world during an election period, for years the voting method had been mail-in ballots. When the member voted, he filled out a paper ballot, selecting his candidates, and placed the ballot in a sealed, unmarked envelope. The envelope was then placed in a second envelope, which had a serial number and a space for the member's signature to confirm it came from the member.

On Election Day, the outside envelope was verified as being from the member by signature and confirmed that only one ballot was received from that member, as indicated by the serial number. Then, the envelope was opened, and the inner envelope was placed in a ballot box to be counted once all the envelopes had been opened. The outer envelope was placed in a separate box for record-keeping.

How to Get an Honest Union Election was perhaps the single most important document the MAD Committee had because it served as the roadmap for ensuring the next election would be fair and honest. To paraphrase Admiral Yamamoto after the attack on Pearl Harbor, Gene DeFries had awakened a sleeping giant.

Chapter 5

Suddenly Susan

> *No group of individuals did more for establishing our country than the American Merchant Seamen and Privateers. Their record speaks eloquently of their devotion and sacrifices.*
> PRESIDENT JOHN ADAMS

★ GENE DEFRIES not only followed in Jesse Calhoon's footsteps as union president, but he also stepped into the political arena. When George H. W. Bush was running for president, MEBA, led by DeFries, helped develop his maritime policy.

When he won the presidential election in 1988, DeFries hosted a pre-inaugural tribute welcoming the new Secretary of Labor, Elizabeth Dole, and the new Secretary of Transportation, Samuel K. Skimmer, to their new posts in the Bush Administration. Elizabeth Dole was Senator Bob Dole's wife, and MEBA had made campaign contributions to Senator Dole over the years. That had provided DeFries with access to the Senate, but now he would have access to President Bush's cabinet. The union newspaper, the *Marine Journal*

(January-February 1989), was filled with photos of DeFries standing with Elizabeth Dole and Sam Skinner.

In February 1990, shortly after Bush's inauguration, a union member named Nick Hadju (pronounced HAY-do) brought a protest to the U.S. Labor Department. The investigating officer was highly interested in the facts being presented; however, within a week, the investigating officer informed Hajdu that the Labor Department would be dropping the case. He would no longer have contact with him.

Elizabeth Dole, now the Secretary of Labor, was very familiar with Gene DeFries. If that was not enough, DeFries had promoted Mr. David Keene to be a public relations man for the union. Keene was the campaign manager for Sen. Dole's unsuccessful bid to become the 1988 Republican candidate for President of the United States. Although there was no hard evidence that DeFries had used his influence to kill the Labor Department investigation, many union members believed it to be the case.

Other actions by the leadership had been uncovered in the previous months, and the MAD Committee retained a lawyer named Susan Souder. Souder graduated from Georgetown University at the top of her class in law school. Today, members of the MAD Committee are uncertain whether Gordon Ward or Joel Bem found her. Still, all agree that she was an outstanding litigator. According to Don McLendon, MAD treasurer, the MAD Committee members at one meeting reached into their pockets and cumulatively donated a total of $10,000 to retain her. She was initially retained to investigate and possibly file a civil suit in federal court to stop the merger of the MEBA and NMU Pension

Plans that was in progress. They also wanted her to reverse the merger altogether.

On March 18, 1990, less than a year after the merger of MEBA and NMU, Susan filed a twenty-five-page civil lawsuit against MEBA/NMU and six specific members of the union's leadership, including C.E. "Gene" DeFries, Clyde E. Dodson, C.W. "Bill" Daulley, R.F. Schamann, Karl Landgrebe, and Donald Masingo. The lawsuit was filed in the U.S. District Court for the District of Maryland, Civil Action No. R-90-822. Souder laid out several areas of misconduct by the union leadership, including denial of voting rights and misrepresentation of the facts regarding:

1) the MEBA/NMU merger,
2) the severance pay situation,
3) problems with the election of convention delegates, and
4) the merger of the pensions.

The lawsuit provided specific facts concerning how the merger was presented to the membership and outlined how the members would not have voted for the merger if they had known that all along the plan was to merge the pensions. It also pointed out that there was a single *yes* or *no* vote for the merger, even though it contained substantial changes to the constitution and bylaws, as well as the appointment, rather than election, of officers for the new Licensed Division of the MEBA/NMU and the convention delegates for the Licensed Division. One vote, yes or no, for everything.

From start to finish, the voting process lasted only 60 days, despite many members being at sea for much of that time and having substantially less than 60 days to read and understand the merger. Union voting periods typically lasted 90 days to give the sea-going membership time to cast their ballots.

The lawsuit outlined the solicitation of ballots, including the fact that many union members felt intimidated by the leadership and surrendered their ballots for fear of retribution against them. The union bylaws specifically stated that "ballots must be cast by mail to a predetermined depository for safekeeping until the designated time to count the votes."

Union leadership was obtaining marked and unmarked ballots from members during the merger referendum. It also presented the fact that members were surrendering their ballots to union leadership. MEBA officials were including unmarked ballots that *they* had filled out with the other ballots being sent to the depository to be counted. The lawsuit stated that union officials actually "bragged that there was a contest to see which union official could collect the most ballots." The solicitation of ballots was widespread across the country at Atlantic, Gulf, and Pacific Ports.

The lawsuit outlined the material misrepresentations regarding the merger. Although the defendants were aware of the funding differences between the MEBA Pension Trust and the NMU Pension Trust, this information was not made available to the plaintiffs. The lawsuit also claimed that a letter in the *Special Merger Supplement* in the *Marine Journal* (Fall/Winter 1987) stated that all union officials would be "available before the referendum vote to answer any questions members had about specific provisions of the merger." The *Special Merger Supplement* indicated that *all benefit plans* covering the members and officers of both NMU and . . . MEBA would be merged.

When the licensed officers expressed concern, they were assured that only the *administration* of the pension trusts would be merged, not the trust funds themselves. The lawsuit included an affidavit by Alex Shandrowsky stating he was assured specifically by Gene DeFries that the pension trusts would not be merged and that DeFries and other MEBA officials knew this was false. Had the members known the truth, they never would have voted for the merger.

Next was the issue of severance pay. The lawsuit outlined how Gene DeFries, Clyde Dodson, C.W. "Bill" Daulley, R.F. Schamann, and Donald Masingo voted themselves a total of over $2 million in severance pay when the MEBA became the MEBA/NMU, even though they retained essentially the same jobs in the same offices. The DEC had passed a resolution shortly before the merger, allowing members of the DEC to receive severance pay if the MEBA was merged with another union.

The lawsuit highlighted that the payments were unauthorized and that the severance pay resolution had never been disclosed to the membership. The resolution was not in the meeting minutes, and the controller was instructed not to disclose the severance payments. The severance pay was considered embezzlement.

As previously stated, a slate of convention delegates was elected during the regular election for District 1 officers. A national convention was then held after the district election, where the elected convention delegates voted for the National

MEBA officers and the NEC. This process is similar to the U.S. presidential election, where each state determines which candidate receives the most votes and then sends delegates to the Electoral College, which elects the president.

Because the convention delegates are included on the ballot for the District 1 officer elections, Susan Souder alleged they were also subject to solicitation and collection of marked and unmarked ballots by certain MEBA officials. DeFries and the DEC not only controlled the vote for MEBA District 1 officers but also controlled the convention delegate vote, thereby controlling the election of officers to the National MEBA—the umbrella organization for MEBA District 1, MEBA District 2, and MEBA District 3 (Radio Operators).

The lawsuit outlined the steps to merge the MEBA and NMU pensions. It stated that the union leadership had filed the application with the Pension Benefit Guaranty Corporation, and that the members were not notified of the plan. The members found out in late 1989, months after the application was filed.

The lawsuit also stated that when the membership in Seattle found out, they voted overwhelmingly, by resolution, to put approval for the merger of the Pension Trusts to a referendum vote by the full membership. This resolution was repeated in San Francisco and was overwhelmingly supported once again. The response on the East Coast was quite different. MEBA officials in Baltimore and New York refused to even allow the resolution to come to a vote.

Furthermore, the lawsuit further stated that the participants and beneficiaries would receive no benefit from the merging of the pension trusts. The merger was for the benefit of the *employer sponsors of the NMU Pension Trust.* In other words, the merger of the pensions was for the benefit of the NMU, not the MEBA. The interests of the NMU Pension Trust conflicted with the interests of the MEBA Pension Trust.

The defendants induced the NMU to merge with MEBA District 1 by promising to use the over-funding of the MEBA Pension Trust to help the ailing NMU Pension Trust after the unions were merged. It was the proverbial carrot on the stick. The MEBA/NMU merger would benefit the NMU Pension Trust on one side and provide generous severance pay on the other.

Finally, the lawsuit claimed that since Gene DeFries became president, MEBA officials had been coercing people applying for pension benefits in the form of a lump sum buyout into making significant contributions to the Political Action Committees (PACs) affiliated with MEBA District 1.

The twenty-five-page document ended with nine counts against the defendants. The charges included:

- Solicitation and collection of ballots.
- Misrepresentation that there would be no merger of the pension assets. Failure to provide full information about the pension trusts.
- Requiring a single yes or no vote that included not only the merger but also changes to the constitution and bylaws, and the appointment of union officials and convention delegates.
- Violation of the defendant's fiduciary responsibilities with respect to the pension trust.

- Voting themselves the severance payments.
- Converting portions of the lump sum pension distribution to benefit PACs.
- Racketeering.
- Mail fraud.

The plaintiffs requested that:

- The merger be declared invalid.
- The 1989 election of convention delegates be declared invalid.
- The defendants be removed as trustees of the MEBA Pension Trust.
- The defendants be removed from their elected positions in the MEBA.
- The defendants pay monetary damages.

A copy of the lawsuit was mailed to Elizabeth Dole, Secretary of Labor, and Nicholas Brady, Secretary of the Treasury.

Despite the inaction by the Department of Labor, actions against the union leadership were escalating elsewhere in the federal government. FBI agents were contacting MEBA members to discuss the soliciting of ballots by the union leadership and asking to interview them at the FBI offices.

They were asked if anyone in the union halls had asked them for their ballots. If they had been asked, the FBI wanted to know whether or not the individual requesting the ballot was in direct communication with Gene DeFries and the DEC. Apparently, the FBI had been notified of the racketeering, voter fraud, mail fraud, and misappropriation of union funds, and they had opened their own investigation. The Department of Labor may have ignored the possibility of illegal union activities. However, the FBI and the Department of Justice took it very seriously.

Chapter 6

In a Flash ... Gordon

> *Unless we have a merchant marine,*
> *Our navy, if called upon for offensive or defensive*
> *work, is going to be most defective.*
> PRESIDENT WILLIAM HOWARD TAFT'S
> INAUGURAL ADDRESS, 1909

★ ONE AFTERNOON IN early 1990, Gordon Ward called Larry O'Toole. In their phone conversation, O'Toole and Ward discussed the idea that the only way to stop the merger of the pension trusts was to reverse the merger between MEBA and NMU and revert to the previous status quo. One way to reverse the merger was to run a slate of opposition candidates in the next union election and gain control of the Licensed Division. If those who opposed the merger became part of the elected union leadership, they would be in a position to reverse the merger of the two unions.

They had a long conversation about how to accomplish this, and Ward asked O'Toole if he wanted to be chairman of the Licensed Division. O'Toole wanted to fight the good fight but wasn't interested in being chairman. The next day, Ward called back and told O'Toole that *he* would run for chairman of the Licensed Division.

In June 1990, the MAD Committee assembled a slate of engineers to run for the officer positions in the MEBA Licensed Division. They would run against the current officers, who had been appointed, not elected, as part of the all-encompassing *yes* vote for the merger in 1987. Ward ran for Licensed Division Chairman and New York Branch Agent. Joel Bem ran for Licensed Division vice-chairman and San Francisco Branch Agent. Nick Haydu ran for Director and New Orleans Branch Agent. Alex Shandrowsky ran for Director and Baltimore Branch Agent. Mark Austin ran for Director and Seattle Branch Agent. Bill Langley ran for Wilmington (California) Branch Agent and one of the convention delegate positions. Larry O'Toole and Louie Coulson also ran for convention delegate positions.

The MAD candidates were running against four of the six defendants named in the civil suit. Gene DeFries was president of MEBA/NMU and chose not to run for re-election as chairman of the Licensed Division. Instead, DeFries chose one of his subordinates, Clyde Dodson, to run for chairman of the Licensed Division.

Gordon Ward and Joel Bem made a good team; they resembled Captain Kirk and Mr. Spock on the Starship Enterprise. Like Captain Kirk, Ward was a man who had a set of values but also had a sense of humor. He was easy to get along with but had no problem walking across the street to tell someone who had dropped some litter to pick it up and keep our city clean. Like Mr. Spock, Joel Bem was a more serious man. He was highly educated and looked at things analytically. As a lawyer, he understood what the MAD Committee could and couldn't do to win the fight. The difference between their personalities was evident in the page-long resumes that each candidate wrote for the *MAD Journal* (October/November 1990). They explained why they were running and what they stood for.

Ward wrote about what was going on and how we, as members of the union, should fight to protect it. He explained that, like many members, at first he thought some sour-grape types posted the stories about the union leadership. When he started asking questions, he found out that the current leadership was lining their pockets with union money and running the union for their own financial gain. He referred to the dictatorial way the union meetings were being run and the secretive communist-style central control of the DEC. It would take a large organization to stop them, and the MAD Committee was ready to lead the way with the assistance of the union membership.

The incumbents had betrayed the membership. They wanted you to believe that Jesse Calhoon had done nothing right for the union. Ward wrote a brief recap of the severance pay and the Alternative Lump Sum Buyout. Finally, he pointed out that although he was not an expert in everything, he did have management experience, graduate-level business courses, marine engineering experience, teaching experience in marine engineering, and extensive exposure to union activities.

While Ward's page read like a letter to the membership, Joel Bem was more specific. His page read like a report, and he used bullet points to list his commitments to the union, most of which referred to preserving or restoring items such as control and democracy. Bem listed several items, identifying some as fact, others as possibility, and others as opinion. He concentrated more on the past practices of ballot solicitation by the union officials, warning the membership, *"That was then, and this is now."* He pointed out that you could actually read the ballot through the outer envelope and then explained exactly how to do it using a 100-watt light bulb so that you could see it for yourself.

Bem also cited legal cases and precedents. He explained that the MAD Committee had asked a federal court to issue an injunction against ballot solicitation. Judge Nickerson agreed with the plaintiffs and stated, "If there is wrongful conduct in the election, and the plaintiffs will certainly be monitoring it, the plaintiffs may resort to the specific Title IV remedies and set aside the election if necessary." Like Kirk and Spock, each man had a distinct personality, yet they seemed to work well together toward the common goal.

The war was on, and Gene DeFries did what any politician would do: He denied that he ever planned to merge the pensions, even though the documents were on file with the government and the minutes of the trustees' meeting contained his instructions to implement the merger. On July 27th, DeFries sent a letter to the membership stating, "Now there will be no merger of the two plans."

Joel Bem made it clear that while DeFries had stopped the merger for now, if the MAD slate was not elected, it would just be a matter of time before DeFries reinstated the merger procedure. The only way to stop the merger forever was to elect the entire MAD slate and send the Slick Slate packing. The MAD committee nicknamed the opposition the "Slick Slate," because whenever they distributed campaign materials, they were published on glossy (or slick) paper rather than standard 20# paper.

Members of the Federation of Public Employees (FOPE), a division of MEBA, were able to vote for branch agents and patrolmen in the MEBA. But they could not vote to choose their own District 1 representatives. They were seeking an autonomous affiliation with the MEBA to gain control of their own union. The MAD slate supported this move, but DeFries was against it because he could dilute the MEBA membership's voting power by including the FOPE membership in the mix. Walter Browne, president of FOPE, was siding with the MAD Committee.

The *Slick Slate* began sending out a series of documents called The MEBA Fact Sheet, which were not at all factual. According to Fact Sheet #5 from the MEBA Team, the MAD Committee was allegedly formed during a secret meeting between MEBA District 2 officers and disgruntled former Calhoon MEBA Engineering School instructors to undermine Gene DeFries and MEBA District 1. They claimed that Gordon Ward was recruited by MEBA District 2, the rival union, and not the MAD Committee. They also claimed it was MEBA District 2, and not voluntary contributions from MAD Committee supporters, that raised and spent hundreds of thousands of dollars to undermine MEBA District 1. None of this was true.

In an open letter to the membership, Gilbert LaDana, former instructor and later administrator at the Calhoon MEBA Engineering School, condemned the incumbent leadership, stating that they "were using the MEBA as their own private club," and that "The officials always came first and the members came second, if at all." He stated that Gene DeFries had told him that his only interest as far as the school was concerned was in obtaining certificates.

LaDana also stated that he had worked with many of the MAD Committee members over the years and that they stood for honesty, integrity, and democracy. He ended the letter asking the members to support the MAD Committee both financially and by voting for their slate of officers. A postscript from Roy Luebbe, former director of the school, joined LaDana in endorsing the MAD Committee.

The MAD Committee coordinated with Jesse Calhoon to hold informational meetings away from the union hall to inform the membership of what was going on. Calhoon would attend these meetings to give them credibility, and members would show up because Jesse Calhoon was going to be there. Meetings were held on all three coasts, including New Orleans, Houston, San Francisco, and New York. At each meeting, the MAD Committee hung a banner that read: *The M.A.D. Committee Presents a Meeting with Jesse M. Calhoon, the Former N.M.E.B.A. President.* The MAD Committee had the meetings videotaped, so they could send the tapes to ships around the fleet and keep the working members informed.

According to a videotape of the New York meeting in August 1990, Larry O'Toole was the MC. He opened the meeting with a few facts about the current union leadership and what they had done. He told the membership that he had first seen the Alternative Lump Sum Buyout information in the 1988 *Pension Booklet.* The option of taking your pension as a lump sum buyout and continuing to work was found on page 18 of the booklet. He stated that Clyde Dodson had told him that only 24 union members qualified for the alternative buyout program, 19 sailing engineers and five union officials. The five union officials were the same five who received severance pay as part of the merger. He also pointed out that the Hutley Report, commissioned by the leadership to justify their severance pay, stated that the leadership didn't have to inform the membership about every compensation and that the membership would have been told if they had asked!

O'Toole also told the membership that at the previous National Convention, the MEBA Pension Trust was listed as the current figure (close to $1 billion). When they described the NMU pension, they stated that since 1951 (i.e., for forty years), they had provided $2 billion. They did not state that the NMU Pension Trust was currently underfunded.

Finally, he listed the ABCs of the MAD Committee:

A: Stop the merging of the pensions.
B: Return the severance payment to the general fund.
C: Stop the solicitation of ballots during elections.

O'Toole also pointed out an array of handouts on a table in the back of the room. He asked all the members to take the handouts, read them, and then pass them along to other union members.

Next up was Alex Shandrowsky. He spoke about the Federation of Public Employees (FOPE) and its association with MEBA. The FOPE has 5000 members compared to MEBA's 3500 members; however, MEBA was in control of its union. FOPE wanted to be able to elect its own officials and have its own constitution and bylaws. Shandrowsky promised that the MAD Committee candidates would work with them to accomplish this.

O'Toole introduced Joel Bem. He told the members that Bem graduated first in his class at the U.S. Merchant Marine Academy and then joked that Gordon Ward had graduated *only* third in his class at Maine Maritime.

Bem spoke about the lawsuit filed by Susan Souder in March 1989. Part of the process in any lawsuit is the service process for the lawsuit. A process server delivers papers informing the defendants of the lawsuit, and the lawsuit cannot continue until all the defendants are served. The union leadership (the defendants) dodged the process server for weeks; secretaries would say they weren't in their office, and they wouldn't answer the door at home. In the end, the lawyer had to negotiate terms, extending the time to prepare for the lawsuit to August 3rd, before the last defendants would accept the service. He also told the members that the lawsuit would be expensive and asked those present to contribute to the MAD Committee.

Gordon Ward was next to the podium. He began by stating that he was not against the union; he was against the union leadership. Ward informed the members that the leadership had granted themselves a double increase in the Money Purchase Benefit (MPB) compared to the sailing members. He pointed out that they each had already taken $1 million or more in their Alternative Lump Sum Buyout. When the pensions merged, they would form a *different* pension trust, allowing them to take a second pension from the new plan. Ward also stated that the union officials were running the union for their own benefit; sailing comes second.

The MAD candidates were having trouble getting the complete mailing list of the Licensed Division members so they could mail information. Although he didn't describe it this way, he explained that they were using the six degrees of separation method, asking members they knew to share the contact information they had for their friends and shipmates.

He used the words *organized crime*. Ward ended his speech by telling the members that running the union was not rocket science. He stated that the MAD candidates have the talent, knowledge, education, and background necessary to run the union. They could also handle negotiations, pointing out that the current officials took off the week that the previous contracts terminated.

Finally, Jesse Calhoon took the podium and spoke for over an hour. Facts and figures backed his statements. Calhoon began by stating that the current officials had made contract *requests* rather than contract *demands*. They had not taken precautions against a potential strike. Instead, they were short on the welfare money because they had taken the funds.

He reiterated the MPB issue, clarifying it by saying the current officials had given themselves an increase from 5% to 15%. Only Gene DeFries had taken a 10% MPB increase because his MPB was so large, it was capped at 10% by federal law. He pointed out that from 1985 to 1988, the administration expenses had increased each year. It went from $3 million in 1985 to $7 million in 1986, $10 million in 1987, and $16 million in 1988. At the same time, both the Tanker Contracts and Dry Cargo Contracts were being reduced. He told the members that a strong union requires an informed membership and an honest election.

Calhoon spoke about the recent events in Poland. He didn't go into details because the events had received international attention and were fresh in the minds of U.S. citizens. For those who don't remember, in 1980, an independent labor union, Solidarity, led by Lech Walesa, was formed. The union membership had grown to 10 million by September 1981 and played a central role in the end of communist rule in Poland. Lech Walesa eventually became president of the new democracy.

Next was a question-and-answer period. Someone asked about the new MEBA/NMU Constitution and Bylaws. Calhoon explained that he had read the documents and realized that they mirrored the Collins-Exxon company union documents. The Exxon contracts between the company and the shipboard officers were created by Collins, a professor at Princeton University; thus, the name Collins-Exxon. Exxon was the union leadership, and the ships' officers were the union membership. He pointed out that all the money generated by the Licensed Division was controlled by the District, not the Licensed Division.

Gordon Ward pointed out that the District Executive Committee (DEC) was holding secret meetings and withholding information from the membership. He also stated that under Calhoon, the members could present a resolution at one hall and vote to pass it. If it passed, it would be presented at all the other halls the following month. If it passed with a majority in the other halls, the resolution would be implemented. Under DeFries, the resolution would be rejected because it needed to be submitted three days before the union meeting. Then, if you submitted it three days before the meeting, it would be declared *out of order* at the meeting and would not be considered for a vote. The leadership was doing everything it could to take power away from the membership.

While both sides were making their respective cases for the election of their slate, the next step was mailing the ballots to the membership for the vote in November. The pamphlet, *How to Get an Honest Union Election,* stated that the candidates, or their representatives, could be present any time the ballots were being handled. So a small group of MAD Committee members attended the process for mailing the ballots to the membership. An impartial administrator, Stanley Ruttenberg, was also present to supervise the mailing of the ballots.

While the ballots were being collated for mailing, Alex Shandrowsky, followed by Don McLendon, wandered around a corner and stumbled upon boxes of duplicate ballots, 14,000 duplicate ballots to be exact! Mr. Ruttenberg offered to stop the election immediately, but the MAD Committee candidates decided not to protest and to let the election continue. Mr. Ruttenberg impounded the 14,000 duplicate ballots.

Shortly afterward, Alex Shandrowsky learned that the contract between Crestar Bank (which received the returned ballots and kept them in a depository) and the union required Crestar to keep the union informed of the number of ballots received, which is another violation according to *How to Get an Honest Union Election,* and infringes on the security of the election. In the article, "Ballot Fraud Uncovered, Impartial Administrator Orders New Election," published in October 1990 by the MAD Committee, violations were explained, along with the following information. Stuffing the ballot box becomes simple math if you know how many ballots have already been received.

Shandrowsky sent a letter of protest to Gene DeFries and Mr. Ruttenberg. A week later, he received a reply from Gene DeFries stating, "I have received your letter of October 11, 1990. I can assure you that your fears, as usual, are unfounded." At the same time, the MAD Committee received word that some FOPE members had received two identical ballots, with the exact control numbers and identical addresses, within a week of each other. They had also been mailed from the same mailing service, through the same postage meter.

Mr. Ruttenberg called for a meeting to be held on October 30, 1990, requesting that both Gene DeFries and Gordon Ward attend with their representatives. On the appointed day, the MAD committee candidates attended, but neither DeFries nor his lawyers were there. The MAD Committee candidates and Mr. Ruttenberg agreed that new gold-colored ballots would be mailed to each member, and the election date would be pushed forward one month from November 30, 1990, to December 31, 1990. He required that the contract with Crestor be amended to prevent them from informing the union of the number of ballots received. He also added procedures whereby he would accompany and inspect ballots when they were moved from the post office to the depository.

Mr. Ruttenberg then discredited the most recent MEBA Fact Sheet (#4), which gave the DeFries version of how the duplicate ballots came into being. (Refer to "Ballot Fraud Uncovered, Impartial Administrator Orders New Election," published October 1990, mentioned earlier in this chapter.) As Joel Bem said, "Liars lie." The MAD Committee sent out a document with copies of the letter from Mr. Ruttenberg as well as letters from other respected individuals, such as Jesse Calhoon, condemning the action by the incumbents, and requesting that members, "Be sure to photostat your ballot and envelope as proof of how you really voted in this election."

On December 31, 1990, New Year's Eve, the new ballots were counted, and the MAD candidates not only defeated every incumbent but also won 11 of 15 convention delegate positions. The *Journal of Commerce*, in its January 1991 issue, reported that Gordon Ward defeated Clyde Dodson in the race for chairman of the Licensed Division by a margin of 1,410 to 992 (58.7% to 41.3%).

Unfortunately, Gene DeFries still held higher offices: President of MEBA/NMU, chairman of the DEC, President of National MEBA, and chairman of the NEC. He still maintained a position of power because he controlled the two tiers above the Licensed Division and Chairman Gordon Ward.

The MAD Committee had won the battle, but the war raged on. One could compare it to the war between Russia and Ukraine. DeFries had immense power and used it authoritatively; he didn't care what the membership wanted. By comparison, the MAD Committee had the heart, drive, and democracy needed to win the war. They had to win; otherwise, their over-funded pension trust would eventually be decimated.

Portrait of Jesse Calhoon when he started sailing, circa 1943. Photo: Courtesy of Curtis Calhoon

Photo of Jesse Calhoon as a licensed engineer, WWII. Photo: Courtesy of Curtis Calhoon

President Richard M. Nixon and Calhoon, meeting at the White House. Photo: Courtesy of Curtis Calhoon

President Ronald Reagan and Calhoon meet at a function. Photo: Courtesey of Curtis Calhoon

With President Reagan, who is signing a bill at the White House. Calhoon stands fifth from the left. Photo: Courtesy of Curtis Calhoon.

Calhoon stands with President Reagan. Photo: Courtesy of Curtis Calhoon.

Portrait of C. E. DeFries. Photo: Courtesy of MEBA

DeFries (left) at Jesse Calhoon's retirement. Photo: Courtesy of MEBA

Shannon Wall, NMU President, w. Gene Defries. Photo: Courtesy of MEBA

DeFries with Secretary of Labor, Elizabeth Dole. Photo: Courtesy of MEBA

DeFries with Senator Bob Dole (R-KS). Photo: Courtesy of MEBA

Left to Right: Joel Bern, Gordon Ward, Alex Shandrowsky Photo: Courtesy of Larry O'Toole

Taken at the "honest" election, Licensed Division Election count, December 31, 1990. Photo: Courtesy of Larry O'Toole

Dinner the night of the election (l to r) Mike Blakeslee, Jack Ricketts, Tom Leahy, Larry O'Toole, Gordon Ward, Victoria Ward, Pete Acaturo. Photo: Courtesy of Larry O'Toole

MAD Committee members celebrate in the Licensed Division office in Washington, D.C. Headquarters on January 1, 1991 (l to r) Jack Rickets, Pete Acaturo, Mike Blakeslee, Larry O'Toole (in the party hat), Carol O'Toole, Gordon Ward, Nick Hajdu. Photo: Courtesy of Larry O'Toole

MAD Committee Members celebrate in the Washington, D.C. Headquarters conference room, January 1, 1991. (l to r) Pete Acaturo, Tom Leahy, Mike Blakeslee, Gordon Ward, Larry O'Toole, Jack Ricketts and Nick Hajdu. Photo Courtesy of Larry O'Toole

96 – DAVID WHITELEY

Gordon Ward and Nick Hajdu discover bags of shredded documents in the Washington, D.C. Headquarters on January 1, 1991. Photo: Courtesy of Larry O'Toole

(l to r) Larry O'Toole, Gordon Ward, Bill Langley and Joel Bem at a meeting on October 29, 1991. Photo: Courtesy of Larry O'Toole

The MEBA union hall in Houston, 2024. The hall was unchanged since the author's first visit in 1980. Photo: Courtesy of David Whiteley

The Houston dispatcher would list all the available jobs on this Sailing Board and members would bid on jobs that they wanted during Job Call at 1:00 pm each day. Photo: Courtesy of David Whiteley

Chapter 7

Dog Catches Car

> *You guys put your ass on the line every day!*
> *Those of us old timers know and*
> *appreciate what you did!*
> COLONEL PAUL W. TIBBETS
> PILOT OF THE ENOLA GAY

(Author's Note: As I researched the newspaper articles and legal briefs, I was sometimes confused because they would write about the District and the Division. District. Division. District. Division. The District is MEBA/NMU District 1 (DeFries et al.). The division is the Licensed Division (Gordon Ward et al.). If you feel confused or overwhelmed when you read this chapter, imagine how the MAD Committee felt living it.)

★ IT WAS NEW Year's Eve, and while most people were celebrating the New Year, Gordon Ward, Nick Hajdu, Larry O'Toole, and others were celebrating their victory against the incumbents and their hopes to bring the union back to its former glory. They were in Washington, D.C., for the counting of ballots and the election results. They thought it would be a suitable setting to celebrate in Gordon Ward's new office in the MEBA/NMU headquarters down the street. Finally, they had one of their own working as the chairman of the Licensed Division with an office in the Washington,

D.C. headquarters and with it, access to all the key people and information in Headquarters.

When they got to the Headquarters, it was late, and the doors were locked, with a security guard watching the building. The MAD gang, with the help of their lawyer, convinced the security guard to let them in. They had worked so hard and sacrificed so much to get here, but they were finally here, and things were going to change—or so they thought.

The euphoria of winning the election was short-lived. Gene DeFries was still president of the MEBA/NMU, and the Licensed Division was just one *division* of the union, division being the key word. The MAD Committee had won the battle but not the war. DeFries' first act was to transfer the chairman of the Licensed Division's office from Washington, D.C., to the union hall in New York. He justified this by stating that in the election, Gordon Ward had won both chairman of the Licensed Division and branch agent for New York; therefore, he should hold office out of New York.

He would not have direct access to the records at the Washington, D.C. headquarters after all. If that wasn't enough, Ward lived outside of Baltimore, an hour's drive to Washington, D.C., but nearly three hours on the train to New York. The solution was to open a Licensed Division office in Baltimore, near the union hall. The MEBA/NMU was not going to pay for it, so Ward had to make other arrangements. The Seamen's International Union (SIU) had offered a $500,000 line of credit, and although Ward never dipped into it, the fact that the funds were available made it possible for him to lease the space.

As mentioned earlier, the DEC controlled changes in the constitution and bylaws, as well as selecting trustees for the various benefit plans, including the pension trust, but this was for District 1 only. The convention delegates were elected to represent District 1, District 2, and District 3 at the National Convention, similar to the Electoral College system. The membership didn't vote at the National Convention; the convention delegates did. When Jesse Calhoon was president, the MEBA Convention Delegates did not have a one-man, one-vote status. The delegate percentages were weighted based on the amount of dues paid.

Even though District 2 and District 3 combined might have more members, District 1 members made more money and paid more dues; therefore, they had more delegate votes. This weighted system was continued during the merger to give MEBA delegates a greater number of votes than the NMU, despite the NMU having more members. The NMU had twice as many members, but the MEBA made three times the income, so they paid more dues and, therefore, had more votes. DeFries retained this weighted system to maintain power, and now he had to find a way to dilute the MEBA delegates' voting strength.

The best way for DeFries and the DEC to skew the convention delegate vote was to bring affiliate unions into the mix and make them *divisions* of the MEBA/NMU. In doing so, the MEBA Convention Delegates would be diluted at the next National Convention by giving all the new divisions a seat at the convention and their own convention delegates. If DeFries could alter (and control) the number of convention delegates, he would retain control of the DEC at the next convention and pass rules to hogtie the Licensed Division.

According to the District 1 MEBA/NMU memo, "MEBA/NMU Members Vote to Reorganize" from April 1991, DeFries began to rearrange the affiliate unions within the MEBA/NMU. Merging the MEBA and NMU brought the Industrial, Technical, and Professional Employees (ITPE) union into the mix, as ITPE was an affiliate of the NMU. He simply separated them from the Unlicensed Division and created the ITPE Division, with its own set of convention delegates. Next, as reported in the *MAD Northwest*, "Late Breaking News!" article of May 1991, he moved the Professional Airways System Specialists (PASS) from their affiliate status with the MEBA/NMU to their own PASS Division, along with a set of convention delegates.

DeFries had the power to do this through the all-powerful DEC, according to notes from the Special District Convention held in January 1991. By March 1991, instead of two Divisions, Licensed and Unlicensed, the MEBA/NMU had four Divisions, Licensed, Unlicensed, ITPE, and PASS. The breakdown was now:

- Licensed Division: 4,000 seagoing and 5,000 FOPE workers
- Unlicensed Division: 4,000 seagoing members
- ITPE cafeteria workers: 13,000 members
- PASS airport workers: 20,000 members

If this wasn't enough, DeFries still had the Federation of Public Employees (FOPE) in the wings. FOPE was currently included in the Licensed Division and had delegates. It would be difficult to split them into two Divisions. Perhaps he could turn the FOPE against the MAD officials and capture those convention delegates, as well.

The next act by the DEC was to pass a resolution stating that the MEBA/NMU was the legal successor to MEBA District 1 and, therefore, in control of the trustees for the various plans, including the Licensed Division's Pension Plan. The trustees in place as of January 1, 1991—the day after MAD won the election—would remain in place. This action was taken because the Licensed Division, under the leadership of Gordon Ward, had filed a lawsuit to take control of the Licensed Division's Pension Plan. This was reported and documented in the "MAD Committee Alert" in February 1991. The licensed ship's officers were the only people contributing to the plan, and they should be the trustees managing it, not DeFries and his cohorts.

The *Journal of Commerce* reported on February 8, 1991, that a federal judge ruled the Licensed Division could unseat and replace the union trustees of its pension plan. DeFries' response to the lawsuit came from the National Executive Committee (NEC), which represented the National MEBA, the umbrella union over MEBA/NMU (formerly MEBA District 1), MEBA District 2, and MEBA District 3. He passed a National Executive Committee (NEC) resolution giving control of the trustees to each district, as reported in the article "Resolution" from February 1991.

This sent things into disarray because a trustee meeting was scheduled in a few days. The trustees were made up of representatives from both the union and the contracted companies. The contracted companies selected half of the trustees, and the union chose the other half. Gordon Ward arrived with a group of his trustees, claiming that a federal court order was replacing the DeFries trustees. The meeting was held, but decision-making was limited. The employer trustees would only vote on resolutions that *both* groups of union trustees agreed to.

While the fight over trustees was going on, other strategies by Gordon Ward to gain control of the Licensed Division's pension plan were taking place. Before the merger vote back in 1988, Albert Jackson, a member of the NMU, had filed a lawsuit to *stop* the merger, which was later revised to *reverse* the merger. Gordon Ward's next move was to join Albert Jackson in the lawsuit and fight to reverse the merger, as well.

The ships' officers supporting MAD, not just the committee, decided to stop their voluntary contributions to the Political Action Fund (PAF) per a letter by DeFries dated May 10, 1991. DeFries used PAF to grease the political wheels. The Department of Labor had sided with DeFries throughout the merger process and against those who were fighting the merger. Why should the MAD group pay into a fund so DeFries could make contributions to the politicians who turned a blind eye to the merger corruption? These were all small steps; the next step would be a big one.

Using the Licensed Division Bylaws, which were presented to the union membership as part of the yes-or-no merger package, Gordon Ward and the Licensed Division Council (LDC) put forward a series of resolutions to make the following changes:

<u>Article II, Section 7(a)</u>: No individual who received severance payments from District 1—PCD, MEBA is eligible for membership or may retain membership in the Licensed Division.

<u>Article II, Section 7(b)</u>: No Licensed Division member shall be eligible for nomination to or to serve in a paid elective or appointed office, by virtue of his licensed Division membership, in the National MEBA, District 1—MEBA/NMU, or the Licensed Division if he has received or is receiving a pension under any MEBA Pension Plan.

In other words, if you had received a severance package as part of the merger or if you had taken a pension but continued to work, you could no longer be a member in good standing of the Licensed Division.

District 1-MEBA/NMU (DeFries et al.) filed a lawsuit against the Licensed Division (Ward et al.) in the U.S. District Court for the District of Columbia Civil Action No. 91 1662 (TFH). This was to reverse the resolutions that had been approved unanimously on July 5, 1991, by the LDC and approved in a membership vote by a wide margin—3 to 1 for Section 7 (a) and 6 to 1 for Section 7 (b).

Also in July, unable to acquire MEBA/NMU District records directly related to the licensed division, Gordon Ward called a meeting of all the branch agents plus a few other key people, including Jesse Calhoon. The goal was to organize a show of strength against Gene DeFries' control of the Licensed Division records. A group of Licensed Division members and some of their family members, including children, organized a protest at the Washington, D.C. headquarters, both on the street outside and at the eighth-floor offices. The purpose of the gathering at MEBA/NMU headquarters was to gain access to the Licensed Division records, which were maintained in the National Headquarters. Even though he was the Licensed Division chairman, Ward was denied access to the Licensed Division records maintained at the Washington, D.C. headquarters.

As a safety precaution, they enlisted a few off-duty Washington, D.C. police officers. DeFries saw the protesters and ordered his in-house security guards to lock the glass office door. However after a while, Louie Coulson and Helen Smith, one of the few female union members, began rattling the door. The door was locked with a magnetic mechanism. When the door shook, part of the mechanism that had been simply lying in the suspended ceiling above fell, causing the door to unlock. The protesters entered the office, forcibly pushing past the security guards, but were unable to confront DeFries because he had locked himself in his office. Louie Coulson stated in an interview that someone suggested Helen Smith and he leave the building lest they be arrested for damaging property. They left shortly thereafter.

The building is on the edge of the Capitol Grounds, and apparently, DeFries had called the Capitol Police, because after a few minutes, they showed up in full riot gear, ready to arrest the protesters. Washington, D.C. police showed their badges and told them nothing was going on. The Capitol Police left satisfied that the protest was generally peaceful The protesters left after gaining some access to the records.

Satisfied that they had made their point, they were prepared to fight all the way to the end.

Jesse Calhoon had waited down in the lobby, but once the protesters were in the office, he joined them. DeFries was not the only one surprised by what happened. While Calhoon was in the office, he spotted Dan Bickford. Bickford had been supportive of the MAD Committee movement in the early days. When it became apparent that he would not be the MAD Committee's choice for chairman of the Licensed Division, he changed horses and began to support Gene DeFries. Had he been working as a spy for DeFries? The *MAD Journal* reports in its article "The Bickford Twist," from October 1991, that when Calhoon saw Bickford in the Headquarters, he told him, "You're a traitor! Get down on your belly like the serpent that you are and crawl down the hallway. CRAWL!"

No one was physically attacked or injured, but three months later, DeFries wrote a letter to the membership spinning the event as an attempt to "seize power physically by breaking into your District's offices . . . " further claiming that they had "destroyed union property and directed abuse at everyone, including the secretaries and clerical staff." He claimed that one secretary, who had just started working in July, "spent several hours in literal fear for her personal safety." (See "Letter to Membership" written by DeFries in October 1991.)

Ironically, the $100 million building was an asset of the MEBA Pension Trust; the Licensed Division owned the building! Later, a judge ruled that the Licensed Division had the right to enter the building, but in the future, it had to give DeFries advance notice. They were also granted access to the Licensed Division records.

In August, several mid-level members of the Slick Team sent a letter to the seagoing membership of the Licensed Division, essentially stating that if they (Ward et al.) can pass resolutions to remove appointed officers from the Licensed Division Pension Plan, they can also pass resolutions to harm you. They wrote, "Those who seek such power always try to find ways to limit or eliminate the rights of the individual." It is ironic that the team that forced a single yes-or-no vote to approve not only the merger but also changes to the constitution and bylaws, thereby granting them ultimate power, would now be concerned about individual rights. (Again, note DeFries' "Letter to Membership" from 1991.)

The *Marine Journal* created a video entitled the *Marine Journal Video Extra,* which included a segment about "What Really Happened" when the officers of the Licensed Division picketed and eventually broke into the Washington, D.C. offices of the MEBA/NMU. They claimed that the intruders gained entrance and were checking financial records. Still, they did not ask to see the Licensed Division records. The secretaries spoke about how frightened they were, stating that the intruders had blocked the doors and exits.

The video did not mention that off-duty Washington, D.C. police were present to ensure that the situation did not get out of hand. The video showed a photo of boxes stacked in the corner of a hallway. It claimed that the Washington Office had delivered the records to the New York union hall, but the boxes were never opened. The video did not mention that the Licensed Division was being run from an office in Baltimore. Ironically, the newscaster for this segment of the video extra was Dan Bickford.

The war between MEBA/NMU and the Licensed Division was heating up, and now not just trade journals were covering the story. In August 1991, *The Village Voice* also ran a front-page article titled "How to Build a Republican Labor Movement." Under the heading, the article listed four steps:

- Merge a White-Collar Union with a Blue-Collar One.
- Appoint Yourself President Without an Election.
- Surround Yourself with Republican Campaign Operatives.
- Pay Yourself and All Other Union Officers Severance From the Old Unions You Merged—and Rehire Everyone for the New Union.

The article raised issues that most of the union membership was not fully aware of. It explained in great detail why the NMU pension was in the toilet.

Before the late 1960s, everyone traveled overseas by passenger liner; transatlantic airplanes were rare and very expensive. Each passenger liner had hundreds of crewmembers to serve the passengers, and the NMU supplied most of the unlicensed crew on U.S.-flagged ships. The SS *United States,* nicknamed the "Big U," was the largest and fastest passenger ship during the 1950s and 1960s. She was built in 1952, was 990 feet long, and had four engine rooms totaling 241,000 SHP. She had a crew of 1,050 men and women, 760 of whom worked in the steward's department serving the 1,982 passengers in the dining rooms and cleaning the passengers' staterooms. The "Big U" was just one of the many passenger ships transiting the Atlantic and Pacific Oceans.

In 1969, the SS *United States* was taken out of service and retired. A new ocean liner did not replace her; instead, she was being replaced by transcontinental airplanes. The unlicensed crew was laid off and sent back to the NMU union hall to be reassigned to another ship. As the passenger ship fleet diminished, so did the NMU jobs. The union members could transition to cargo ships and tankers. But when the Vietnam War ended in the mid-1970s, those jobs also began to disappear. According to *The Village Voice*, the NMU union members began to retire in larger numbers.

Meanwhile, the available jobs in the NMU shrank from 22,000 in the late 1960s to fewer than 2,000 jobs in 1991. The NMU Pension Plan was paying pensions to 12,000 pensioners. Still, with so few workers paying into the pension, the NMU was paying $50 million a year in pension benefits while taking in only $14 million in pension plan contributions. They needed a bailout, and the MEBA offered the merger of the two unions, including the merger of the two pensions. DeFries knew that the pensions would be merged from day one.

The other situation explained by *The Village Voice* was why the MEBA was a Republican union when Democrats had historically supported unions. They claimed that when Jimmy Carter lost the election in 1980, Jesse Calhoon connected with Ronald Reagan to maintain his foothold in Washington politics. This was partially true, but the union had historically been linked with whoever supported the Jones Act, which protected merchant mariners and their jobs.

President Richard Nixon was a strong supporter of the Jones Act, and the MEBA supported him.

Regardless, Calhoon was connected to Ronald Reagan, so when Gene DeFries became the MEBA president in 1985, he continued to support Reagan. When George H. W. Bush became president in 1988, the MEBA and NMU were in the process of merging, and, as previously stated, DeFries developed close ties to Bush's Secretary of Labor, Elizabeth Dole. Then, when the MAD Committee started filing civil suits and writing letters to the Department of Labor asking for assistance in fighting the corrupt union officials, the Department of Labor turned a deaf ear to MAD. It is believed, but not proven, that DeFries used his influence to keep the Department of Labor out of the fight. According to *The Village Voice*, the unions "handed over well over a million dollars in PAC money to Congress."

The Village Voice article included information on David Keene (previously mentioned), who was initially hired by Jesse Calhoon and retained when DeFries became president. Keene's Republican connections ran back to 1968 when he "came to the attention of columnist and far-right ideologue Pat Buchanan, who referred him to then Vice President Spiro Agnew." He eventually started a lobbying firm that included the Contras (part of the Iran-Contra Affair during the Reagan Administration) and the World Freedom Foundation as clients. Keene was also the campaign manager for Bob Dole's unsuccessful presidential campaigns in 1988 and again in 1996. When Jesse Calhoon retired, DeFries gave David Keene a bigger and more visible role, which influenced and enhanced the union's Republican connections; he was handling public relations.

The article also mentioned that NMU member Albert Jackson had run against the NMU President, Shannon Wall, in 1983. Jackson lost and cried fraud, accusing the union leaders of soliciting ballots. Several mid-level federal officials investigated it and, suspecting that Jackson was correct, recommended that the Labor Department investigate further. However, the top officials at the Labor Department decided that nothing untoward had happened and took no action. The NMU lawyer, in this case, had previously been a Labor Department Solicitor. Coincidence?

In August 1991, the MEBA/NMU and the Licensed Division agreed to a temporary truce concerning litigation. By now, eight lawsuits had been filed, five by the Licensed Division and three by the MEBA/NMU, and the court costs were mounting rapidly. The MEBA/NMU was dipping into its working capital to pay for legal expenses. At the same time, the well-paid seagoing Licensed Division was being funded by the membership. Most members were contributing something, but there was a rumor about one member selling his classic car and sending the money to the MAD Committee.

Before it was over, the fight would cost the membership hundreds of thousands of dollars. A MAD Committee financial report, dated through January 1991—when Gordon Ward was voted Licensed Division chairman—showed that invoices from January 1990 to January 1991 totaled $160,314.19.

Both sides were making resolutions and taking other actions in an attempt to stop the opposition. Money was always an issue on both sides. Joel Bem wrote a letter to the MEBA/NMU requesting the quarterly financial reports. The quarterly reports had always been distributed to the various union halls across the country and made available to the membership; however, now the financial statements were no longer being distributed. The distribution stopped in January 1991, when the MAD slate won the election. Bem suspected that the leadership was using dues money provided by the Licensed Division to fight the Licensed Division, and he wanted to see the quarterly reports to confirm it.

DeFries was trying to increase the power of the NMU, ITPE, and PASS against the Licensed Division. In retaliation, Gordon Ward and the LDC amended the bylaws to prevent the vice presidents of those divisions from having the ability to run for office in the Licensed Division, which would further dilute the power of the Licensed Division.

What DeFries didn't think about until much later was that one of the newly formed divisions was linked to the NMU. While the Licensed Division was losing convention delegate strength, the NMU was gaining convention delegate strength and would be able to take control of the DEC. They would achieve this by replacing MEBA-based officials with NMU-based ones and pushing MEBA into the background, which could ultimately be worse for Gene DeFries.

In September 1991, the *Marine Officer* wrote an article titled "Appeals Court Rules" and reported that the court ruling that granted the Licensed Division the right to appoint trustees to the MEBA Benefit Plans was upheld by the Court of Appeals, 4th district. Now the Licensed Division benefits would be managed jointly by trustees appointed by the

Licensed Division and trustees selected by the contracted companies; DeFries would have no control over the MEBA Benefit Plans, including the pension plan.

Ward seemed to be gaining momentum, and in October, DeFries requested mediation of all the outstanding lawsuits. The response from the MAD lawyer, Susan Souder, was that the Licensed Division would agree to arbitration, not mediation. Why? Because 1) arbitration is binding, 2) it takes place in front of a judge, and 3) the judge's decision is final. One side wins with no appeal. By comparison, mediation is held by a mediator, who may or may not have a legal background, and the mediator usually finds a compromise between the parties, not a clear win or loss. The Licensed Division had no choice but to continue the litigation. Susan responded by writing the "Letter to Michael D. Derby, Esq." dated October 1991, stating that the DEC's desire was "to delay and obfuscate the real issues between parties."

Gene DeFries had one more card to play; he needed to get the FOPE on his side for the final dilution of the Licensed Division's delegates at the National Convention. In the summer of 1991, DeFries used the power of the DEC to establish a new union hall, and with it, he appointed the branch agent.

The new hall would be located in Fort Lauderdale, Florida, and he appointed Alexander "Doc" Cullison as the branch agent. Conveniently, the Fort Lauderdale union hall would be located in the same building that houses the FOPE. Doc Cullison was the branch agent for Houston and was defeated in the previous election by MAD candidate Steve Scott. Cullison, a loyal DeFries supporter, needed a job. Besides locating the hall next to the FOPE, DeFries hired a security company, Asset Protection Team, to protect the union hall and the membership. The Asset Protection Team was a union-busting agency, similar to Pinkerton.

Gordon Ward sent a letter to the membership on October 25, 1991, explaining how Alex Shandrowsky went to the Fort Lauderdale union hall and was accompanied on the elevator by two sizeable individuals in shirts with the MEBA logo. When he got off the elevator, he was met by a larger contingent wearing similar MEBA shirts. Shandrowsky, a Director in the Licensed Division and the Baltimore branch agent, was entitled to visit another union hall. Still, he described the encounter as a hostile situation. Gordon Ward ended the letter by stating that he had asked Gene DeFries to dismantle their fort and return the hall to a typical working atmosphere.

In November 1991, "Circus Rally at Fort Lauderdale," a document produced by the MAD committee, stated that the following action by DeFries to curry favor with the FOPE was a meeting led by Doc Cullison, with Gene DeFries sitting behind the podium. Gordon Ward and several MAD Committee members were present, as well as the entire Federation staff and, of course, the FOPE membership. Six Asset Protection Team personnel were also there providing security. Gordon Ward got up to speak at the podium, and within seconds, his microphone was cut off. Doc Cullison popped up behind the podium with a working microphone and started leading the FOPE members in chants, drowning out Gordon's speech.

When it came time for voting on resolutions, they would skip the *Whereas* paragraphs and just read the *Therefore be it Resolved* paragraphs. It didn't matter because the resolutions were presented on color-coded paper, and the FOPE membership was instructed to vote *no* for those resolutions on pink paper and *yes* for those resolutions on blue paper. Coincidentally, all the Licensed Division resolutions were on pink paper, and all the FOPE resolutions were on blue paper.

Near the end of the meeting, Gene DeFries took the podium and told the crowd that he found only one fault with the meeting; there just wasn't enough good food. He then promised to rectify that and pay for a real spread of good food at the next meeting. One of the FOPE stewards told the MAD group that he didn't want to "hear any shit" from them because Gene DeFries "is our man."

Gordon Ward's response to Doc Cullison and his relationship with the FOPE was to remove him as the Fort Lauderdale branch agent and replace him with Paul Krupa, who held a First Assistant Engineer's license and had worked as Ward's administrative assistant.

On November 26, 1991, Paul Krupa was assaulted in a hallway just outside the union's office by two men identified as Joe Gambino and his son, who were thought to live in the Fort Lauderdale area. Members of the Asset Protection Team stood by and took no protective action during the assault. Paul was taken to the Broward County Hospital Emergency Room and treated for injuries to his right shoulder, neck, and back, as reported in December 1991 by District 1—MEBA/NMU in the article "MEBA Union Representative

Assaulted." Ironically, DeFries was paying over $100,000 per month out of Licensed Division union dues for the Asset Protection Team, which took no action to protect Branch Agent Paul Krupa.

As a result of Paul Krupa being attacked, on January 2, 1992, the Licensed Division moved the Fort Lauderdale union hall out of the same building as the FOPE and into a new union hall located closer to Port Everglades, where most of the ships docked, to protect their membership from any further assaults.

It was reported in the *Marine Officer*, "Federal Judge Blasts Merger Language," November 1991, that Judge Griesa, a Federal District Judge in Manhattan, ordered the MEBA/NMU to rewrite a summary of the merger agreement in plain English, further stating, "I went to college, and I went to Law School, and I can't understand this." This was about the lawsuit brought by Albert Jackson, the NMU member, and later joined by Gordon Ward, to overturn the merger. The judge was shocked by the MEBA/NMU document's poor writing and ordered a revised version that the rank-and-file membership could understand. The purpose of the lawsuit was to call for another vote to either reaffirm or dissolve the merger. Gordon Ward believed that Gene DeFries was doing whatever was necessary to delay the vote.

The lawsuits filed by the Licensed Division were all in Baltimore, whereas those filed by MEBA/NMU were in Washington, D.C. In November, the Licensed Division made a formal request to the Federal District Court for the District of Columbia to combine all the court cases in the Baltimore court, since all the cases were so closely related. Furthermore, they requested that Judge William M. Nickerson preside over all the cases because he had already heard some of the cases and was familiar with many of the fundamental issues, some of which were simply duplicates filed in different court districts. By placing all the court cases under one judge in one court district, some essentially identical cases were also combined into a single case. Only the *Albert Jackson vs. NMU* case to invalidate the merger would continue to be held before Judge Griesa in the Federal District Court for the Southern District of New York.

The next significant step by Gene DeFries occurred on December 16, 1991, in his "Call For Special District Convention" letter, which he announced would be held on January 16, 1992. He had asked the Department of Labor for an opinion on the legality of candidate eligibility restrictions and the voting strength formula based on dues paid rather than one-man, one-vote, even though *he* was the man who had initiated *both* policies in question.

The Department of Labor sent an opinion letter in December 1991 by John Depenbrock titled "U.S. Department of Labor Letter," stating that both rules violated LMRDA laws. DeFries called for the convention to make the necessary corrections. The convention would address:

- Making null and void amendments passed by the Licensed Division.
- Introduce a trustee amendment to the MEBA/NMU Constitution.
- A referendum vote on whether the merger should be reaffirmed or dissolved.

- Correct the voting strength by division to "one-man, one-vote."

Under the new rules outlined in "Voting Strength at the District Convention," the convention delegates' voting strength formula for each division would shift:

- Licensed Division   42 to 31
- Unlicensed Division 27 to 19
- ITPE   6 to 44
- PASS   25 to 6

The new voting strength formula would be used to vote on whether to have a referendum on the merger.

Gene DeFries had just outsmarted himself. In his attempt to dilute the voting strength of the Licensed Division, he had substantially increased the voting strength of the Unlicensed Division and ITPE, which was split from the NMU. Yes, the Licensed Division would lose its voting power; it would be transferred to the NMU with a nearly two-thirds majority!

As the year came to a close, December was a busy month. DeFries had lost control of the Licensed Division Pension Plan in court and on appeal. His next step was to appeal to the U.S. Supreme Court, requesting the right to control the Licensed Division's Pension Plan.

When Judge Griesa learned of the Special District Convention scheduled for January, he issued a Stipulation of Discontinuance in the U.S. District Court, Southern District of New York (No. 88 Civ. 1682 (TPG), requesting that the parties put the lawsuit on hold until the conclusion of the convention and abide by the referendum on whether to reaffirm or dissolve the merger.

Susan Souder, lawyer for the Licensed Division, respectfully declined because the voting strength would be different from the voting strength of the original merger vote. She requested that only the original MEBA members and the original NMU members be allowed to vote to reaffirm or dissolve the merger, since the ITPE and PASS were not involved in the original merger vote. Each union would vote again, just as they had in the original vote. If either union voted to dissolve the merger, it would be terminated. Judge Griesa agreed and issued a revised Stipulation of Discontinuance. The convention would be held on January 16, 1992, followed by a merger vote by the former MEBA and the former NMU membership.

Lucille Hart, Plans Administrator for the Benefit Plans, issued a letter on December 20, 1991, stating that the 6% dues would not be deducted from vacation checks for Licensed Division employment beginning in 1992. Gordon Ward had devised another method to cut off the funds provided by the Licensed Division, which the MEBA/NMU District would use to pay for their lawyers to fight the Licensed Division.

Gene DeFries challenged the decision to stop paying the 6% union dues. However, Ward pointed out that the constitution allowed members to opt out of deducting the money from their vacation checks, as long as the 6% payment was made by the first day of the following quarter. This action would halt the flow of vacation dues money to the MEBA/NMU and the DEC until April 1, 1992, significantly impacting their cash flow; they would be unable to use Licensed Division dues to pay lawyers fighting the Licensed Division.

Albert Jackson's lawyer, Arthur Fox, sent a letter to the MEBA/NMU lawyers requesting that Albert Jackson be provided with a complete mailing list of all members for the referendum vote for the merger. He also requested that if the MEBA/NMU published information in the *Marine Journal* extolling the virtues of the merger, Jackson be granted equal time in the publication, meaning equal space on the pages. Furthermore, if the MEBA/NMU leadership were attending a union meeting, he requested the date, time, and place, so he could also attend. The letter aimed to ensure that the MEBA/NMU was granting equal time, and if not, they would have the opportunity to demonstrate to Judge Griesa which side was playing fair.

Nearly one year after Gordon Ward had won the election, he reported in the "Federation of Public Employees Letter" dated December 1991, that under the leadership of Doc Cullison, the FOPE was losing membership to competing unions, such as the Fraternal Order of Police. He further recommended that Walter Browne be reinstated as the president of FOPE in the hopes of saving the union.

By the end of 1991, a combined total of eleven civil lawsuits had been filed by both sides. One or two of the cases had already been settled, and many of the cases were combined, as recommended, but the fight continued.

Chapter 8

Enough!

> *As the sea is beautiful not only in calm,*
> *but also in a storm,*
> *so is happiness found not only in peace,*
> *but also in strife.*
> IVAN PANIN

★ THE SPECIAL DISTRICT Convention, scheduled to take place in Fort Lauderdale, Florida, on January 16, 1992, had not been stopped by either Gordon Ward or the courts. The sole purpose of the convention was to further constrain, if not crush, the Licensed Division and Gordon Ward. On January 6, 1992, Ward sent a letter to the DEC stating that the convention should not be held. However, if it were held, the first order of business should be the vote to dissolve the merger. Unfortunately, there was no response, and the Special District Convention was going to be held as scheduled.

On January 15, 1992, one day before the Special District Convention was scheduled to begin, the Licensed Division Council (LDC), led by Gordon Ward, unanimously passed a resolution declaring the merger of MEBA and NMU to be dissolved. The former Licensed Division shall now be known once again as MEBA District 1. The resolution also stated that a referendum vote would be held beginning March 1, 1992, to determine if the MEBA District 1 membership wanted to affiliate with NMU, ITPE, and/or PASS. If the membership voted to affiliate with any of the other unions, MEBA District 1 would negotiate the merger with those unions and put the merger agreement to a vote by the membership. By doing this, all or part of the MEBA/NMU merger could be reaffirmed by the MEBA membership if they desired. Finally, the resolution called for an election of officers for the MEBA District 1 in September 1992.

Until the election scheduled in September, the officials of the new MEBA District 1 would be:

Gordon Ward—President
Alex Shandrowsky—Vice President, Atlantic Coast
Nick Hajdu—Vice President, Gulf Coast
Mark Austin—Vice President, West Coast
Joel E. Bem—Secretary/Treasurer

The resolution was presented to the membership for a vote, and it passed 823 to 46 (92.5% to 7.5%). The *D1 PCD Bulletin* published this critical information in "District No. 1—PCD, MEBA Instituted" in January 1992. The merger creating the Licensed Division was officially dissolved, and the Licensed Division was now known once again as MEBA District 1.

A letter of support for the dissolution of the merger was sent to MEBA District 1, signed by several maritime union leaders, including the presidents of MM&P, MEBA District 2, and SIU, indicating that this was good for the maritime industry.

The Special District Convention was held on January 16th, as scheduled, and about 50 MEBA District 1 members picketed outside. As suspected, the Licensed Division Convention Delegates were diluted, and the NMU/ITPE delegates represented 63% of the total delegates. In comparison, the Licensed Division would have had only 30% of the total delegates. The NMU/ITPE dominated the convention.

While the Special District Convention was in progress, Gordon Ward notified the contracted companies that the Licensed Division had assumed its pre-merger status and that, in the future, MEBA District 1 would supply all licensed manpower and handle all future negotiations. Furthermore, as reported in the *D1 PCD Bulletin*, January 1992, action would be taken against any company that attempted to continue performing those functions with the MEBA/NMU.

On Friday, January 17th, the convention announced that it was placing the Licensed Division into emergency trusteeship, and Gene DeFries named Alexander "Doc" Cullison as the Licensed Division trustee. Ward responded via fax that "We don't know over whom you are imposing this trusteeship, but it is not us." The Licensed Division no longer existed, and it became obvious that it had been dissolved just in time; the trusteeship had been DeFries' plan all along. The *D1 PCD Bulletin* published an article on January 17, 1992, with this headline

"DeFries Puts Organization that Doesn't Exist Into Trusteeship"

That same day, a group of thirty MEBA District 1 union members moved into the Portland Hall, which was not one of the major union halls. Al Camelio was appointed as the new Portland representative, replacing Bill Fast. Fast brought in security guards, but with thirty members standing together, they were not intimidated, as was the case in other halls. Fast demanded that each member sign a document stating they were duty-bound to abide by the MEBA/NMU Constitution, a pledge of loyalty to DeFries, in order to receive any kind of service in the Portland Hall, but they all refused.

The following day, Saturday, January 18th, volunteers moved into each union hall and set up a 24-hour presence to protect the halls. They learned that the locks in the Seattle hall had already been changed on January 16th, the day before the trusteeship was officially announced, in anticipation of Doc Cullison's takeover.

Five days after the Special District Convention began, DeFries was well aware that the Licensed Division had returned to the original MEBA District 1. In an attempt to regain control of the licensed officers, he tried to take over the Norfolk Union Hall, another of the minor halls, and use it for back-door shipping by establishing a telephone shipping operation. The *D1 PCD Bulletin* published an article on January 21, 1992, titled "DeFries Back Door Shipping Operation Foiled."

When the MEBA delegation arrived, Norfolk Branch Agent John Delullo attempted to attack Alex Shandrowsky with a billy club but was stopped by the MEBA members. The police were called but left when they realized that Shandrowsky was the branch agent for Baltimore and the Atlantic Coast Vice President and was entitled to be in the Norfolk Hall.

Later that day, Fred Schamann and Doc Cullison showed up, and that evening the police returned. Alex Shandrowsky was arrested for trespassing, a misdemeanor. The police offered to arrest Doc Cullison on the same charge if Shandrowsky wanted to press charges, but he refused to stoop to their level. Alex was released on bail later that night. Larry O'Toole was arrested at the same time but was not charged.

The next day, Gordon Ward showed up with Paul Krupa and berated Fred Schamann, who was acting as the MEBA/NMU branch agent. He then appointed Krupa as acting branch agent for MEBA District 1. The MEBA District 1 members set up picket lines outside the hall. Krupa, using new technology called a cellular telephone (remember, it's 1992), set up communications and held the daily job call on the sidewalk in the rain. Shortly after the job call, a van with several Asset Protection Team security guards pulled up. They were still trying to protect Gene DeFries' MEBA/NMU from the newly established MEBA District 1.

The MEBA continued to ship members in Norfolk from the street in front of the union hall using a cell phone. Seagoing members of the MM&P and the SIU joined the picket lines. The MEBA/NMU was having difficulties operating the Norfolk Hall because the other local unions, including the local phone company and UPS, would not cross the picket lines.

Despite Doc Cullison's letter to major shipping companies advising that the MEBA/NMU had placed the Licensed Division into trusteeship with him as the trustee, by the end of January, only one job, a night relief job, had been approved. It was shipped by MEBA/NMU in the Portland Hall before it was secured by the MEBA rank-and-file. All other seagoing jobs were being shipped through MEBA District 1. The *D1 PCD Bulletin* reported these events in "The Week's Events in Summary," January 25, 1992.

By the end of February, Joel Bem had provided the membership with a financial report outlining where they were and where they were going, with MEBA District 1 separated from Gene DeFries' MEBA/NMU. He reported that with the help and support of the membership, MEBA District 1 was up and running under its own power in a very short period of time. He reported that new accounts had been opened and a professional accounting firm had been retained. Bem also stated that the membership had been paying their dues, some in advance, directly to MEBA District 1.

MEBA accepted a $500,000 loan from the SIU to ensure that it could pay all the bills. Some members were disappointed that the once-wealthiest maritime union had to borrow money. But with DeFries out of the way, they expected a quick recovery. The good news was that, due to prudent management, none of the loan funds had been used at the time the financial report was issued. Joel Bem also promised the return of a Quarterly District Financial Report as had been a past practice, which he provided in the "Summary—Financial Report" on February 28, 1992.

Gene DeFries was not going to go away quietly. He still planned to hold a referendum to reaffirm the merger between MEBA District 1 and the NMU. Ballots had been distributed and would be counted on March 27, 1992. As expected, there were many flaws in DeFries' referendum vote. To begin with, he would not allow the votes of the marine engineers and deck officers to be counted because on January 15th, they had declared the merger void and stopped paying dues, so they were not members in good standing. The vote was being conducted in less than 60 days, making it difficult for members at sea to cast their ballots.

Then there were the usual procedures that one would expect from a DeFries-managed vote. Members in one hall were given pencils and not allowed to mark their ballots with pens. Although the standard voting method had been by mail, this time, collection boxes were placed at some FOPE job sites. FOPE employees were also called to a special meeting and instructed to "bring your ballots." This vote also included thousands of ITPE and PASS employees who were not members of the original MEBA or NMU and had not voted for the original merger.

By comparison, in Gordon Ward's "Situation Update" article from February 1992, the MEBA District 1 vote, scheduled to begin on March 1, was supervised by the American Arbitration Association. Members had ninety days to cast their votes. Votes were counted on June 2, 1992. Only members who were eligible to vote in the 1988 merger were allowed to vote again this time.

Another major event occurred on March 1, 1992, when C.E. "Gene" DeFries announced his resignation as President of what remained of District 1 MEBA/NMU and the National MEBA. Alexander "Doc" Cullison was tapped to replace DeFries as head of the MEBA/NMU and President of the NMEBA—the umbrella that covered District 1, District 2, and District 3. Young appointees also replaced the Vice President and Treasurer of the MEBA/NMU. DeFries was planning a quiet retirement, but the FBI had been investigating the activities orchestrated by DeFries and his cohorts for the last two years, and they had other ideas.

The 102nd National Convention, where the elected convention delegates would vote for members of the National Executive Committee (NEC), as well as several resolutions, was scheduled for March 1992. The District 1 Convention Delegates would also vote for members of the District Executive Committee. Gordon Ward, Joel Bem, Alex Shandrowsky, Nick Hajdu, and Mark Austin were all elected to the DEC. Gordon Ward was elected President of the NMEBA, replacing Doc Cullison. Ward and Joel Bem were elected to the NEC along with members of District 2 and District 3.

Convention delegates passed a resolution that rescinded amendments related to the merger adopted at the 1988 National Convention, as well as another resolution that substituted MEBA District 1 for District 1 MEBA/NMU. They passed a resolution that recognized the NMU as an unlicensed union, as it existed before the merger. They passed a resolution terminating immediately the services of the Asset Protection Team.

Resolutions expunging MEBA/NMU from the National MEBA were not the only thing they voted on. They passed a resolution opposing the Secondary Registry, a practice known as "flag of convenience," which allowed cheap foreign labor from third-world countries to man European merchant ships.

The U.S. Congress had passed legislation that would replace all radio operators on merchant ships with an automated Global Maritime Distress and Safety System (GMDSS) by 1998. The convention delegates passed a resolution supporting onboard maintenance of electronic equipment by a licensed electronics officer, which would give radio operators an opportunity to remain aboard ships in a modified capacity. Ironically, prior to 1998, the only officer that was required by law to be onboard before a ship could sail was the radio operator. Now he was being replaced by automation.

The vote by the membership to determine if they wanted to affiliate with the NMU, ITPE, or PASS was concluded in June, and the membership voted not to affiliate with any of them. In September, the membership formally elected Gordon Ward, Joel Bem, and all the others to the leadership positions they held after the Licensed Division voted to dissolve the merger and revert to their original MEBA District 1. The union was back to its original configuration, and the MAD Committee had saved the membership from losing their pension benefits.

Chapter 9

Back to the Future

> Throughout American history,
> the Merchant Marine has been indispensable
> to our security and prosperity.
> PRESIDENT LYNDON B. JOHNSON

★ MEBA DISTRICT 1 was unmerged from the MEBA/NMU, but some loose ends needed to be resolved, and the courts were still in the mix. One major issue to be resolved was financial. The MEBA/NMU's lawyers requested permission to withdraw from an outstanding lawsuit because they were still owed over $1 million for previous work. Furthermore, the MEBA/NMU owed over $100,000 in back rent for their Jersey City headquarters, and the landlord was asking the state court to force payment. When the MEBA District 1 members voted to unmerge the unions, they took their money with them, and the MEBA/NMU could no longer siphon off funds.

Susan Souder was still the MEBA District 1 lawyer and was working to settle all the disputes between the MEBA District 1 and the MEBA/NMU. On June 4, 1993, an Interim Agreement was reached titled "Interim Agreement for Settlement of Disputes Between District 1 MEBA/NMU and

District 1 MEBA." In the agreement, all pending litigation initiated by either party would be dismissed *with prejudice*, meaning it would be permanently dismissed. Any internal union charges made against either Gordon Ward or Doc Cullison would also be dropped.

The agreement also stated that the merger was terminated and that the MBEA/NMU would be restructured by the National MEBA into six autonomous divisions:

- District 1—MEBA
- District 2—AMO (American Maritime Officers, formerly MEBA District 2)
- District 3—Radio Electronics Officers Union
- District 4—NMU/MEBA
- District 5—ITPE/MEBA
- District 6—PASS/MEBA

The National MEBA's NEC would be restructured, and the president of each new division would be a member of the *Interim* NEC. In the interim, Gordon Ward would be president of the NEC, and an election for national officers of a new NEC would take place no later than March 1994. Until the election, the Interim NEC could not place any of the districts into trusteeship. The Interim NEC would also convene a National Constitutional Convention no later than March 1994 to draft a revised constitution. The Interim Agreement also allowed any district to secede from the NMEBA upon a 60% vote by the district's members.

All the assets owned by the MEBA District 1 before the merger would be returned to it. This included the Norfolk

Hall and the Peach Orchard Estate, where the Calhoon MEBA Engineering School had been relocated. Likewise, the assets formerly owned by the NMU would be returned to it.

An expense fund was created where outstanding money would be placed in the fund and then distributed according to the terms outlined in the agreement. For example, if the severance pay lawsuit was settled before June 30, 1993, MEBA District 1 would receive the proceeds; however, after June 30, the proceeds would be deposited into the Expense Fund. The agreement also outlined specific procedures for payment from the Expense Fund.

Most importantly, the agreement removed the National MEBA from the MEBA District 1 Pension Plan, required all disputes to be submitted to binding arbitration, and, although it was signed by all parties, required approval by a majority vote from the membership, in lieu of a costly and time-consuming referendum.

In February 1994, the AMO voted overwhelmingly to secede from the National MEBA and become an independent union. During the same time period, the Federation of Public Employees (FOPE) considered becoming affiliated with MEBA District 1 instead of being a division of it. On April 9, 1994, FOPE affiliated with MEBA District 1 and became the National Federation of Public and Private Employees. Since that time, the National Federation has grown dramatically.

Gordon Ward had worked so hard to dissolve the merger and save the MEBA Pension Plan; clearly, he had experienced many sleepless nights and was exhausted. He later wrote about the financial sacrifices he made. He had paid for much of his air travel, postage, and phone calls out of his own pocket, and he had taken time off from his chief engineer's job during the campaign. After he was elected, his salary as chairman of the Licensed Division was less than he had earned as a chief engineer.

The Department of Justice was dealing with former union leadership, and there was really nothing else to do. Ward announced his retirement in April 1994, well before his term as union president was up and shortly before the 1994 contract negotiations would begin for tankers and dry cargo ships. The negotiations can be challenging under any circumstances. Seemingly, he had accomplished his goal of saving the pension and needed a rest.

The DEC selected Joel Bem to replace Gordon Ward as president and would finish the term. He was selected because, although he was the secretary-treasurer and not one of the three vice presidents, the vice presidents were located on each of the coasts, while Bem was working in the Washington, D.C. headquarters alongside Ward. Under the circumstances, he was the likely successor.

Bem was tasked with contract negotiations at a time when the contracted companies had to deal with changes in government subsidies and maritime laws. Some U.S.-flagged companies were starting to shift from the U.S. flag to "flag of convenience" status and sought major concessions, including pay cuts and reductions in benefits. They were asking for as much as a 60% total reduction. MEBA District 1 was just coming out of a battle to regain its independence from the MEBA/NMU and had a completely new leadership entering into the negotiations. Many of the contracted companies stood together and negotiated as a group against both MEBA

District 1 and NMU, which was once again operating independently of MEBA.

As a result, some concessions were made under the new long-term contracts, and most, if not all, of the jobs were saved. Despite concessions, the contracts were still better than either the contracts signed in 1984, under Jesse Calhoon, or the contracts for the competing union, the AMO. If contract negotiations were not challenging enough, the AMO's separation from the National MEBA meant they also lost their affiliation with the AFL-CIO. While they no longer had the AFL-CIO's support, they also did not have to follow any AFL-CIO rules. Among other things, the AFL-CIO had rules about raiding another union's contracts.

After the Tanker and Dry Cargo contracts had been settled, the LNG contract was still in negotiations. Energy Transportation Corporation (ETC) was unique because it was the only LNG fleet under the U.S. flag, and its union contract was negotiated independently of the other contracted companies. The LNG contract had two unique features: the company had the *right of selection*, which meant that ETC could hire or fire anyone as long as the billet was filled with a MEBA union member. The LNG contract also included a no-strike clause, preventing them from going on strike, and thus making arbitration the last method of negotiation.

Starting in December 1994 and continuing through July 1995, MEBA District 1 and ETC went into binding arbitration over their contract negotiations. ETC had "demanded draconian concessions in the economic package aggregating to nearly 40%," according to President Joel Bem, who published "Arbitration Award Energy Transportation

Corporation " in July 1995. The representatives for ETC claimed that the contracts for delivering LNG to Japan would begin to expire starting in 1997.

If there were no contract renewal, the ETC fleet would not be able to compete in the highly competitive world market because the ship's officers were among the highest paid in the world. Also, they would be competing with LNG ships operating under a "flag of convenience." MEBA countered that the contracts would likely be extended, and asking for cuts in pay and benefits was premature. ETC, on the other hand, wanted cuts based on potential future developments.

ETC sought to eliminate the Cost of Living Allowance (COLA), which adjusted wages based on inflation, and reduce the vacation time from day-for-day to 20-for-30 for the master and chief engineer, and 18-for-30 for all other officers. This would result in less vacation time than the unlicensed crew received. They wanted to pay overtime based on a 56-hour workweek, rather than a 40-hour workweek.

In a previous contract, air travel had been reduced from first class to business class or better, which amounted to business class on the international legs and first class domestically. Now, they wanted to reduce air travel from business class to coach. Imagine 22 hours of travel, including layovers and sitting in coach seats, followed by 12 hours of work after only 8 hours of jet-lagged rest.

Thanks to the lawyer, Richard Hirn, and the MEBA union officials, including MEBA Engineering School Director Larry O'Toole, "The Arbitrator's decision denies ETC virtually every request for concessions in their proposal." The arbitrator eliminated any pay increases or COLA for the contract's three-year duration, according to arbitrator Charlotte Gold's ruling, "Arbitration Between District 1 MEBA and Energy Transportation Corp." on July 4, 1995.

The contract negotiations became the major topic in the 1995 MEBA elections, scheduled for the end of 1995. Running for election began in August. When the members began running for office, the MAD Committee members separated into two groups: those who were willing to accept concessions in order to keep their jobs and those who were upset about making significant concessions in the last contract negotiations. Joel Bem and his team were the more moderate candidates. They referred to themselves as the MORE team (**M**EBA **O**fficers **R**e-Election campaign).

Alex Shandrowsky and his MEBA 95 team believed they could negotiate more effectively. Jesse Calhoon had been a mentor and friend to Shandrowsky even before the MAD Committee, and Shandrowsky, like Jesse Calhoon, was more inclined to demand better wages and benefits rather than make concessions.

A third Candidate, Durwin Davis, who was a former Houston patrolman, also ran for president. He was one of the DeFries team that lost their job in the 1990 election and ran his campaign referring to the MAD Committee as *Madmen*. For some unknown reason, he also used his campaign material to criticize openly the person who was First Lady at the time, Hillary Clinton.

The union became polarized, similar to Republicans and Democrats, with one side supporting Joel Bem and the other supporting Alex Shandrowsky. Like other elections, much of the campaign material consisted of negative ads. Gordon

Ward wrote an eight-page document titled "1995 MEBA Election Comments II" (undated) to the membership, criticizing Joel Bem as being weak and indecisive. He was critical of the contract negotiations in which Bem had managed to save the jobs by agreeing to certain concessions in pay and benefits.

Joel Bem responded by pointing out that the union was facing the loss of good jobs if the contracted companies reflagged the vessels to a flag of convenience. He also pointed out that his team had been successful in limiting the concessions requested in the ETC arbitration; all they lost was the COLA. Joel Bem pointed out that Jesse Calhoon had filed two lawsuits against the MEBA to prevent them from "exercising any advantages over the AMO and SIU (the unlicensed union affiliated with AMO)," and Calhoon was endorsing Alex Shandrowsky.

As previously stated, Jesse Calhoon had been mentoring Shandrowsky for years, and Alex Shandrowsky shared Calhoon's views on tough negotiations and no givebacks. In the documents supporting Joel Bem, the common thread was that Bem had done a great job, and that Shandrowsky was not being truthful. Shandrowsky was thought by some to be a disgruntled MAD supporter. Larry O'Toole also wrote and signed a two-page letter (undated) in support of Joel Bem and against Alex Shandrowsky. It was noted in the letter that Susan Souder said of Gordon Ward's eight-page letter, "It is filled with lies." O'Toole offered anyone who wanted more information to visit him at his home or call him. His address and phone number were posted at the bottom of the letter.

The voting ended on November 30, 1995, and ballots were counted on December 4, 1995. The final result was that Alex Shandrowsky and the MEBA 95 team defeated Joel Bem and the MORE Team, and Shandrowsky became president on December 31, 1995.

While the election was taking place, Joel Bem was negotiating with Hvide and VanOmmeren Shipping to man new ships being built. The contract would have created 184 new jobs for the MEBA-licensed officers on ten new ships being built and three ships that were being purchased. When Hvide and VanOmmeren Shipping found out that an election was taking place, the company's lawyers called headquarters to find out who had won the election. When they found out that the incumbents had lost, they would not continue with the contracts unless the president-elect approved of them.

Shandrowsky reviewed the contract, and the companies were informed that the new president of MEBA District 1 did not want the contract. Hvide and VanOmmeren Shipping signed contracts with the AMO and SIU within two days, according to an unsigned document titled "Are We Better Off Now?" (see subsection "Hvide") written in April 1996. The Conclusion section of the same article noted that under the Shandrowsky administration, it was alleged that he was going to "run the union just as Jesse Calhoon did, with the exception of collecting ballots." He was also accused of terminating anyone who was not aligned with him.

The first MEBA Benefits Plan trustees meeting under the new MEBA administration took place within 90 days of the election, in March 1996. At the meeting, Lucille Hart was put to a vote to terminate her services. Lucille Hart had been the pension plan administrator for decades. The pension plan had become fully funded under her leadership and was currently valued at more than $1 billion. The trustees consist of equal numbers of union trustees and employer trustees.

The union trustees voted unanimously to terminate Hart, while the employer trustees voted unanimously to retain her. Following the deadlock, Lucille Hart decided to resign. The union trustees also insisted that Larry O'Toole resign. This was documented in a letter from T. E. Murphy, President of Marine Personnel & Provisioning, Inc., to James MacGillivray, dated March 20, 1996.

O'Toole had transformed the Calhoon MEBA Engineering School (one of the union's benefits) into an outstanding institution, but the union trustees wanted him out. So, he decided it would be in the best interest of the union if he resigned. O'Toole remained at the school for six months to effect a smooth transition.

O'Toole went back to the union hall and took a job as a third assistant engineer on the Sailing Jobs board. He also worked as a third assistant engineer aboard the LNG *Libra* for four months. Ironically, he started as a second assistant on the LNG *Aquarius* in 1977 and rose to chief engineer within the ETC fleet. Twenty years later, he was not too proud to take a third assistant's job. He later stated that, by comparison, it was somewhat relaxing to be a third assistant after so many years of stress as a chief engineer.

One year later, on March 22, 1997, the Association for Union Democracy held a celebration dinner for Herman Benson. Although Larry O'Toole was no longer director of the school, he was asked to give a speech honoring Benson. He spoke about how Herman Benson and the AUD had provided invaluable information in the fight to take back the MEBA and the pension. According to O'Toole, although Benson and the AUD represented all unions, he was wearing a jacket at the celebration dinner emblazoned with a MEBA logo; the merger fight was that significant to him.

Chapter 10

Trials and Tribulations

> *The American Merchant Marine—*
> *Indispensable to Our Freedom.*
> PRESIDENT HARRY S. TRUMAN

★ BILL CLINTON WON the election for President of the United States in 1992 and was inaugurated on January 21, 1993. As with all new presidents, Clinton appointed his own cabinet members, including Secretary of Labor Robert Reich and Attorney General Janet Reno, who oversaw the Department of Justice and the FBI. With Elizabeth Dole no longer the Secretary of Labor, MEBA District 1 could at least hope for a more balanced approach toward any criminal indictments of the former MEBA/NMU leadership. Thankfully, this was soon to come.

The membership learned that, based on FBI and Labor Department investigations, as well as a grand jury recommendation, on June 30, 1993, the Department of Justice indicted Gene DeFries, Alexander "Doc" Cullison, and several other members of the union, including low-ranking members, on federal charges. (See U.S. Court of Appeals, District of Columbia Circuit, No. 94-3110, Argued December 13, 1994.)

C.E. "Gene DeFries, Clyde Dodson, Reinhold F. "Fred" Schamann, Claude W. "Bill" Daulley, and Donald K. Masingo were all charged with racketeering, organizing an illegal enterprise to gain control over the union, soliciting and collecting unsealed ballots, and embezzling union funds (the severance package).

Alexander C. "Doc" Cullison, late to the game, was only charged with racketeering, organizing an illegal enterprise to obtain control over the union, and soliciting and collecting unsealed ballots, but not charged with embezzling union funds.

In addition to the above charges, DeFries, Schamann, Masingo, and nine low-level union employees were charged with mail fraud. Cullison and Masingo were accused of extortion. Karl Landgrebe had died and was not charged.

The trial was scheduled for 1994, and the initial hearings for the criminal case against Gene DeFries and other union leaders occurred in May 1994. They claimed that the charges of mail fraud should be dismissed because their actions were not illegal. The first part of their claim was that the impartial administrator monitored the elections, and it was his responsibility to ensure that the ballots were handled properly. The union leadership had no duty or obligation to ensure that the ballots were handled properly. The court disagreed with this argument.

The second argument was that the act was not chargeable as mail fraud because there was no money or property involved. The mail fraud statutes require that the illegal action was committed to obtain another person's money or property. Lawyers claimed the ballots couldn't be considered "property" for mail fraud, as they were only paper and therefore intangible. The government filed an interlocutory appeal, arguing that the ballots belonged to the union members, regardless of their size, and that the right to vote was integral to their livelihood, thus constituting a form of compensation.

Judge Jackson did not immediately decide on the motions. Instead, he canceled the July 11th trial date and postponed the trial until January 23, 1995. On January 13, 1995, ten days before the trial was scheduled to begin, the U.S. District Court of Appeals for the District of Columbia ruled that the mail fraud counts should be reinstated, which meant that Gene DeFries (et al.) would stand trial on all counts (as noted in the MEBA District 1 Memorandum, *HQ*—94-008, June 3, 1994).

On December 16, 1994, approximately a month before the trial was scheduled to begin, Don Masingo, the former branch agent for Baltimore and Director of the Licensed Division of the MEBA/NMU, pleaded guilty to the racketeering charges. As part of his plea agreement, he was required to pay back the $249,000 (plus interest) he had taken as part of the severance package. He also pleaded guilty to the charge of conspiracy to defraud the government. The conspiracy charge was based on Masingo's assistance in approving over $230,000 in fraudulent expense reimbursements, which allowed other union officials to receive their salaries tax-free by labeling them as business expenses. Masingo also agreed to fully cooperate with the government as part of his plea deal (according to a MEBA press release titled "Union Official Pleads Guilty in Marine Engineers Beneficial Assn. Case," December 16, 1994).

The maximum penalty for the RICO conspiracy charge would be up to 20 years in prison plus a $250,000 fine or double the amount of the proceeds from the offense, whichever is higher. The penalty for the conspiracy charge would be up to 5 years in prison plus up to a $250,000 fine. Worse than that, the sentences could run consecutively. Masingo was 67 years old and would almost certainly die in prison if the maximum sentences were imposed.

The court case began on January 23, 1995, as scheduled. Tampering with ballots was at the heart of the government's case. Severance pay was the other major component in the case. The government contended that the defendants gained and maintained their union offices, for which they were paid salaries, based on the elections in 1984, 1987, and 1990. The evidence showed that the elections were fraught with ballot tampering by the defendants and their agents. The defendants claimed that, based on the margin of victory in the elections, even if all the tainted ballots were discarded, the total tallies would not have altered the outcome of the election.

The government argued that a rule requiring the government to prove that an alternate outcome would have ensued in an untainted election would make it virtually impossible to challenge the victors. The government did prove that ballot-tampering was endemic in every hall across the country. In short, "the elections were a sham and a charade, and were rendered so by the defendants' corrupt practices."

On July 6, 1995, DeFries, Dodson, Cullison, Daulley, and Schamann were found guilty on all counts by the jury, as reported in a MEBA press release titled "Maritime Union Officials Convicted on Racketeering Charges," July 6, 1995.

Ironically, the motion for forfeiture of salaries and severance payments took place on December 7, 1995, the anniversary of the bombing of Pearl Harbor. (See the case, United States v. DeFries, 909 F. Supp. 13 (D.D.C. 1995), December 7, 1995.)

Under the RICO statutes, the penalty for election-tampering that provided the defendants with employment was forfeiture of their salaries between 1985 and 1990. This situation included not only the MEBA and later the MEBA/NMU salaries but also the National MEBA salaries for those years. Any defendant who had also received a severance payment was required to forfeit that payment, as well. Essentially, the defendants would lose every penny they had earned from 1985 to 1990.

Besides forfeiting salaries, Gene DeFries was sentenced to 60 months (five years) in prison, and Clyde Dodson was sentenced to 57 months (four years and nine months) in prison. C.W. "Bill" Daulley was sentenced to 21 months in prison. DeFries, Dodson, and Daulley planned to appeal the verdict. Alexander "Doc" Cullison and Fred Schamann accepted their guilty verdicts. They agreed to cooperate with the prosecution regarding the low-level union employees, who were tried separately. Cullison was required to pay restitution of $114,520.10, and Schamann was required to pay restitution of $385,399.71. District 1 MEBA v. Travelers Casualty and Surety Co., No. 00-CV-737, September 27, 2001, outlines the case. The court also ordered that the availability of the defendants' assets would be preserved during the appeals process to satisfy the orders of forfeiture.

On September 12, 1997, the United States Court of Appeals for the District of Columbia Circuit began hearing the appeals of Gene DeFries and Clyde Dodson. (USA v. DeFries, Clayton E., No. 96-3015 and No. 96-3016). Claude W. "Bill" Daulley passed away the day before oral arguments began and, as a result, his appeal was dismissed. Other defendants had been separated from these three men by the district court because a committee of six union officials, these three men from the MEBA and three others from the NMU, had been the responsible committee for governing the new MEBA/NMU.

The appellants based their appeal on technicalities, not on the fact that they had not committed the offense for which they were found guilty, one year and nine months before the appeal. One of the technicalities was the jury selection, which the appellants claimed was tainted. They argued that the percentages of white and black voters in the area were disproportionate to the percentages of the general population of the jury pool. The white jurors were underrepresented in violation of the Sixth Amendment. The white population constitutes roughly one-third of the total population, but the white jurors constituted only about twenty-three percent of the jury.

According to the government, the appellants forfeited their chance to challenge the jury selection by waiting too long. The district court had denied the jury selection motions in the original trial, and the appellate court upheld the court's ruling.

The next issue addressed by the appeals court was jurisdiction over the 1988 merger referendum mail fraud count. The appeals court had allowed the district court to proceed with the mail fraud count. The issue presented by the defendants was that the mail fraud statutes require that the people were defrauded to obtain either property or money.

The mail contained ballots, which are neither property nor money; they were just paper. The government contended that the paper was, in fact, the property of the union members and represented their income (money).

The problem was that when the appeals court overturned the district court's decision to dismiss the mail fraud issue, its written decision came after the trial had begun. In the appeal, the appellants argued that the mandate issued by the appeals court occurred after the trial had begun; therefore, the district court lacked jurisdiction to proceed in this matter. The appeals court agreed with the appellants, and the 1988 merger referendum mail fraud count was dismissed on this technicality.

Still under appeal were the 1989 and 1990 Election Mail Fraud counts. The key difference was that in 1988, Congress broadened mail fraud statutes to protect honest services, alongside money and property. Hence, the 1988 merger was under the initial statutes, but the 1989 and 1990 elections fell under the revised statutes.

The decision of the appeals court regarding mail fraud was based on the jury instructions provided by the district court. The jury instructions listed seven possible violations, including soliciting and collecting unsealed ballots and voting them in favor of the defendants' interests. Others included obtaining duplicate ballots and using the U.S. mail to send and receive duplicate ballots, among other issues. While six possible violations were all violations of the statutes, soliciting ballots in favor of the defendant's interests was technically not a violation. Since the district court's jury instructions didn't specify that *all* of the possible violations needed to be considered, it was possible that the jury could have convicted on just the first violation, in favor of the defendant's interests, which was not a mail fraud crime unto itself. For this reason, the appeals court reversed the appellants' mail fraud convictions.

Embezzlement was the subsequent appeal. DeFries (et al.) had authorized severance payments for themselves as part of the merger. They argued that under the old constitution, they were authorized to establish compensation levels for all union officers and employees unless otherwise directed by a vote of the membership.

The government argued that DeFries had actually taken steps to conceal the severance payments from the membership, specifically by failing to include them in the minutes for the meeting where the severance package was approved and then directing the union's controller not to reveal any details of the plan. They also pointed out that when the membership did eventually find out, the MAD Committee filed suit to recover the money. Since the membership did not authorize the appellants to take the money, the appeals court did not decide on this issue.

The next argument by the appellants was that they had taken the severance payments based on advice of counsel. Their lawyers had advised them that the severance package was perfectly legal, and they moved forward in good faith based on that information. If, in fact, it was illegal, then it was the lawyer's fault, not theirs. They further argued that the jury had been given improper instructions regarding the advice of their lawyers; the jury should have been instructed that good-faith reliance was a defense against embezzlement.

The government countered that the appellants were not entirely forthcoming with the facts of the severance package; the lawyer had advised them to take a smaller amount equal to one month's pay for every year of work. Ultimately, the appeals court deemed the jury instructions related to the advice-of-counsel defense to be inadequate, and the convictions for severance payments were reversed.

The appeals court then turned its attention to the RICO charges. These racketeering charges were based on the fact that leaders of the MEBA District 1 and the NMU worked together and conspired to create a single union (MEBA/NMU) that would ultimately benefit themselves.

The penalty for the RICO charges included forfeiture of salaries from 1985 to 1990, because that was the "benefit" received from their illegal activities. They would also need to forfeit property purchased with money from the illicit proceeds. The appellants argued that they should be required to repay the net salaries, after taxes, rather than the gross salaries, because the government had already received their taxes. The government argued that the forfeiture was a penalty, not just a return of money acquired from illegal activity, and that the penalty would be forfeitures of the gross salaries.

Finally, the appellant's lawyer argued that the jury instructions for the RICO charges were flawed. Specifically, the jury instructions did not require the government to prove the existence of an enterprise (a conspiracy). Instead, the jury was told that they "should regard the two unions as a single enterprise," which meant that the District court had already determined the existence of an enterprise. Once again, the appellant's lawyers were able to get the conviction reversed based on a technicality in the language of the jury instructions by the district court. The reversal of the RICO convictions also reversed the related forfeiture of salaries.

The evidence was clear; Gene DeFries and other union officials had worked together to tamper with the ballots to merge the MEBA and NMU, written themselves a severance package without notifying the membership, altered the pension lump sum buyout rules to benefit themselves, and conspired to merge the pensions after promising that they wouldn't. They did not deny any of this, but despite clear evidence, the appeals court had reversed all the district court's convictions. Several reversals were based on technicalities in the language used in the jury instructions.

Regardless of how you feel about Donald Trump's federal trial in 2024 on falsifying business records, the following happened as part of the trial: After the closing arguments, the judge, prosecution lawyers, and defense lawyers held meetings to agree upon the jury instructions before turning them over to the jury. This action seemingly showed the government how to stop appeals using jury instructions, something that didn't occur in Gene DeFries' trial.

After the appeal, MEBA filed a civil restitution action to collect the money embezzled in the form of severance from DeFries and Dodson. They received $403,036.95 from DeFries and $515,000 from Dodson per the District of Columbia Court of Appeals case No. 00-CV-737, decided on September 27, 2001.

In addition to the money, MEBA acquired a 438-acre parcel of farmland located in Florida from Gene DeFries. The land was part of a 1,254.56-acre parcel purchased by Gene DeFries and his wife on March 5, 1991, according to the warranty deed on file. (This information was found in the document *Phase 1 Environmental Assessment* by BCM Engineers, dated November 1998.)

The MEBA District 1 membership (including the activists who had formed the MAD Committee) did not closely follow the federal case filed by the FBI. Gene DeFries was no longer part of the union, and the membership was concentrating on putting the union back on track. The thought that he might go to prison for his crimes was satisfying enough. The end result was that he didn't go to prison, but the district court case and the subsequent appeals court reversal lasted over four years. The team of lawyers that represented Gene DeFries and Clyde Dodson wasn't cheap. The legal fees were almost certainly somewhere in the mid to high six figures and, coupled with the money and property they paid in restitution, significantly affected their personal wealth.

As someone once said, the best way to get back at a rich man is to make him a poor man.

Epilogue

The sea was not meant to be controlled.
The sea was meant to be sailed.
JOHN ACUFF

★ BELOW ARE details on a few book topics that were further developed and may be of interest to the reader. In 1997, Alexander "Doc" Cullison received a PhD. and became Dr. Alexander Cullison. His field of study was labor relations and conflict resolution.

In 1998, since he was no longer director of the school, Larry O'Toole ran against Alex Shandrowsky for president of MEBA and won the election. He was president until 2001, when he retired. Larry and Carol still live on their farm in Connecticut and winter in Florida.

Later, in November 1998, Pronav Ship Management (Pronav), a German-based company, took over the contracts to deliver LNG from Indonesia to Japan, replacing Energy Transportation Corp. (ETC).

The NMU became an autonomous affiliate of the SIU and began discussions for merging the two unlicensed unions in 1999. In August of that same year, Pronav applied to the U.S. Maritime Administration (MARAD) to re-flag all eight LNG ships to the Marshall Islands, a flag of convenience country. Pronav began negotiating revised contracts with MEBA District 1. MEBA wanted to retain all the officers but was willing to work with foreign, unlicensed crews from countries like the Philippines. What the MEBA didn't realize was that the SIU was also negotiating with Pronav. They were offering to remain onboard as the unlicensed crew and bring in the AMO as the officers. The AMO offered to fill the top officer billets with American officers and bring Croatian officers in as watch-standing mates and engineers at roughly 25% of the current pay for American officers.

The LNG fleet was notified via email in March 2000 that the AMO would take the place of MEBA, while the SIU would continue to be used on the LNG ships. Shock among the officers would be an understatement.

Later in September 2000, Pronav re-flagged the LNG *Virgo*, where both Larry O'Toole and the author worked as chief engineers for a combined 20 years, to the Marshall Islands.

On June 3, 2001, the NMU officially merged with the SIU. The administrations were combined, but the pensions remained separate.

Susan Souder took office as an associate judge of the Baltimore County Circuit Court, 3rd Judicial Circuit, in May 2002. She retired on July 3, 2018.

On November 15, 2008, Clayton "Gene" DeFries passed away at his home in Florida. He was 80 years old.

Jesse Calhoon, the longest-serving MEBA president, passed away in 2013. He was 90 years old.

Gordon Ward's former ship, the SS *Puerto Rico*, was renamed the SS *El Faro* in 2006. The *El Faro* was hit by Hurricane Joaquin and, on October 1, 2015, the ship sank on its route between Jacksonville, Florida, and San Juan, Puerto Rico. All 33 crew members were lost.

Herman Benson, Founder of the Association for Union Democracy, died on July 2, 2020, just one week before his 105th birthday.

Most of the primary members of the MAD Committee are still alive. The author is still in contact with Larry O'Toole, Don McLendon, Alex Shandrowsky, and Mark Austin. They are all retired and living comfortably on their union pensions.

Joel Bem is working as a licensed engineer on the training ship, TS Kennedy, at Texas A&M Maritime Academy in Galveston, TX. Part of his job is to educate the cadets concerning the ship's steam propulsion system.

Mark Austin retired from MEBA and is working shore-side with steam boilers.

An election was held in 2021, and all five of the MEBA officials (president, three vice presidents, and secretary-treasurer) were Kings Point graduates. In the 2024 election, four of the five MEBA officials ran for re-election unopposed. The fifth official decided not to run for reelection after over 30 years in the union and was replaced by another Kings Point graduate. *The Kings Pointers must be doing something right!*

It should be noted that the author visited the MEBA hall in Houston in August 2024, and it looked exactly the same as it did 24 years before, when he retired. Today, MEBA has approximately 2,700 members and around 1,300 applicants, totaling roughly 4,000 ships' officers. Upon reviewing the open board (unfilled positions), he discovered that most of the open positions were for first assistant engineers and chief engineers. He was told that third assistant engineers, fresh out of the academy, have a starting salary around $150,000 per year, and chief engineers range from $240,000 to

$320,000 per year. The pension plan remains funded at about $900 million.

Gordon M. Ward passed away at his daughter's home on Father's Day, June 16, 2025. He was 86 years old.

About the Author

★ DAVID WHITELEY grew up in the farmland and foothills of Sussex County, New Jersey. His family had many merchant mariners, including both of his grandfathers, who were licensed marine engineers, and his brother, who also graduated from the U.S. Merchant Marine Academy. So David knows the industry well! He is a Kings Point graduate and has sailed for 25 years. Most of his career was on liquefied natural gas carriers, the most complicated ships in the merchant marine fleet. He sailed for nine years as a chief engineer aboard the LNG Virgo.

David secretly married his wife, Diane, in 1973. This was two years before graduation, and marriage was a dismissal offense at the academy. The day before his marriage, the regulations changed when a midshipman who had been dismissed for being married won his lawsuit. That makes

David the first legally married midshipman from any of the five federal military academies!

The LNG Virgo was re-flagged to a foreign registry, a "flag of convenience," and David was replaced by a crew working for reduced wages. David retired and earned a degree in Design and Development at Sam Houston State University, become a custom home designer specializing in accessible home designs. One of his custom homes earned national recognition. Use the email below to contact David Whiteley: david@whiteleydesign.com

www.ingramcontent.com/pod-product-compliance
Lightning Source LLC
Chambersburg PA
CBHW032050150426
43194CB00006B/478